Broke to Boss

BROKE TO BOSS

First edition. March 2, 2025.

ISBN: 979-8230150459

Written by Killian Drake.

Table of Contents

Dedication

This book is dedicated to every millennial and Gen Z individual who has ever felt the crushing weight of financial insecurity. To those who have juggled multiple side hustles, sacrificed weekends, and endured sleepless nights worrying about money. To those who have questioned their abilities and felt lost in the labyrinth of personal finance. This is for you. Your struggles are not in vain.

Your perseverance is inspiring. This book is a testament to your resilience and a roadmap to a brighter financial future. This is a dedication to the power of self-belief, the importance of relentless effort, and the undeniable truth that financial freedom is not a privilege, but an achievable goal for all who dare to chase it. May these pages empower you, guide you, and ultimately, help you write your own story of financial success, a story far more

compelling and fulfilling than any financial struggle ever was.

Preface

I wrote this book because I've been there. I know firsthand the crippling anxiety of living paycheck to paycheck, the frustration of overwhelming debt, and the hopelessness that can accompany financial instability. I spent years feeling lost and overwhelmed, making mistakes that cost me dearly. But through relentless

learning, strategic planning, and a stubborn refusal to give up, I transformed my own financial situation, going from broke to boss. I didn't do it overnight. It was a challenging journey, filled with both triumphs and setbacks. But the lessons I learned along the way are invaluable, and I'm excited to share them with you. This book isn't just a collection of financial strategies; it's a roadmap based on real-world experience, a guide designed to empower you to take control of your financial future. My hope is that this book will inspire you to take action, to embrace the challenges, and to build a life of financial freedom and abundance. Remember, your financial

journey is unique, but the principles in this book will provide the foundation you need to succeed. Let's build your financial empire, together.

Introduction

The traditional approach to personal finance often feels outdated and irrelevant to the realities faced by Millennials and Gen Z. We're navigating a landscape of student loan debt, gig economies, volatile markets, and an ever-increasing cost of living. The "save early, invest wisely" advice, while true, often feels out of reach when you're struggling to make ends meet. This book takes a different approach. It acknowledges the unique challenges you face and provides practical, actionable strategies tailored to your generation. We'll delve beyond basic budgeting, exploring innovative ways to increase your income, strategically manage debt, and build a robust wealth-building system. We'll cover smart investing strategies that are accessible, even with limited capital, and explore the power of side hustles and entrepreneurial pursuits. This book is not a passive read; it's a call to action, an invitation to take ownership of your financial future. It's time to move beyond simply surviving and start thriving. It's time to build a life you love, on your own terms. Are you ready to become the boss of your own finances? Let's begin.

Assessing Your Current Financial Situation

Let's get real for a second. You're probably here because you're tired of the paycheck-to-paycheck grind. Maybe you're drowning in student loan debt, barely making rent, or constantly stressing about your next purchase. You're not alone. Millions of millennials and Gen Z are facing similar financial struggles, feeling overwhelmed and unsure of how to build a secure financial future. But the good news is, it's possible to turn things around. This book is your

roadmap to financial freedom, and this chapter is the first crucial step: understanding your current financial landscape.

Before we can build a strong financial foundation, we need to know where we stand. This means taking a brutally honest look at your current financial situation. It might feel uncomfortable at first, but trust me, this is the only way to create a realistic plan for the future.

This process involves several key steps:

1. Listing Your Debts:

This might seem obvious, but it's essential to be thorough. Grab a pen and paper (or open a spreadsheet – whatever works best for you). List *every* debt you have: student loans, credit card balances, medical bills, personal loans, payday loans – the works. For each debt, note the following:

Creditor: Who do you owe the money to?

Balance: How much do you owe? Be precise.

Interest Rate: This is crucial. Higher interest rates mean you're paying more in interest over time.

Minimum Payment: What's the minimum monthly payment required?

Due Date: When is the payment due?

This detailed list will give you a clear picture of your overall debt burden. Don't shy away from the numbers, even if they're daunting. Acknowledging the reality of your situation is the first step towards conquering it. For example, let's say you have three credit cards:

Card A: Chase Freedom Unlimited, $2,000 balance, 18% interest, $50 minimum payment, due on the 15th of each month.

Card B: Capital One Quicksilver, $1,000 balance, 21% interest, $30 minimum payment, due on the 10th of each month.

Card C: Discover it, $500 balance, 15% interest, $20 minimum payment, due on the 20th of each month.

Seeing these numbers laid out clearly gives you a powerful starting point. Don't just focus on the total; notice the varying interest rates—that's important for debt repayment strategies we'll discuss later.

2. Calculating Your Income:

Next, we need to determine your monthly income. This isn't just your salary; it includes all sources of income. List everything:

Primary Job: Your main source of income (salary, hourly wage, etc.)

Side Hustles: Any extra income from freelance work, gig jobs, online businesses, or investments. Even small amounts add up. **Other Income:** This could include alimony, child support, rental income, or anything else that contributes to your monthly cash flow.

Be sure to use your *net* income – your income after taxes and deductions. Knowing your exact take-home pay will be crucial for accurate budgeting.

3. Tracking Your Expenses:

This is where many people struggle, but accurate expense tracking is vital. For at least one month, meticulously record every single expense, no matter how small. Use a budgeting app, a spreadsheet, or even a notebook. Categorize your expenses for better

understanding. Common categories include:

Housing: Rent, mortgage, utilities, homeowners insurance.

Transportation: Car payments, gas, public transportation, parking.

Food: Groceries, eating out, coffee.

Debt Payments: The minimum payments on all your debts (refer back to your debt list).

Entertainment: Movies, concerts, subscriptions (Netflix, Spotify, etc.).

Personal Care: Haircuts, toiletries, gym memberships.

Clothing: New clothes, dry cleaning.

Other Expenses: Anything else not included in the above categories.

Remember, honesty is key here. Don't leave anything out, even those seemingly insignificant purchases. A latte a day might seem minor, but those small expenses add up significantly over time.

4. Determining Your Net Worth:

Your net worth is simply the difference between your assets (what you own) and your liabilities (what you owe). To calculate it, you need to list all your assets:

Checking and Savings Accounts: The balances in your bank accounts.

Investments: Stocks, bonds, mutual funds, retirement accounts. **Real Estate:** The value of any property you own (house, apartment, etc.).

Other Assets: Anything else of value you possess (cars, jewelry, collectibles, etc.).

Then, list all your liabilities (your debts) – you've already done this in Step 1. Subtract your total liabilities from your total assets to arrive at your net worth. A positive net worth indicates that your assets exceed your debts; a negative net worth means you owe more than you own.

5. Creating a Realistic Budget:

Now that you have a clearer picture of your income, expenses, and net worth, you can create a realistic budget. There are many different budgeting methods, but the core principle is to ensure your expenses are less than your income. Here are a few popular methods:

The 50/30/20 Rule: Allocate 50% of your income to needs (housing, food, transportation, etc.), 30% to wants (entertainment, dining out, etc.), and 20% to savings and debt repayment. This is a simple and easy-to-understand approach.

Zero-Based Budgeting: Every dollar of your income is assigned a specific purpose, leaving a zero balance at the end of the month. This requires meticulous tracking and planning but provides a great deal of control over your finances.

Envelope System: Assign cash to specific categories in envelopes, and once the cash is gone, that category is maxed out for the month. This forces you to stay within your allocated amounts.

No matter which method you choose, the key is to track your spending against your budget consistently. Regularly reviewing your budget and making adjustments as needed is essential. Don't be afraid to adjust your budget based on your financial goals and lifestyle.

Tools and Resources:

Numerous tools and resources can help you through this process.

Budgeting apps like Mint, Personal Capital, YNAB (You Need A Budget), and EveryDollar can automate much of the tracking and provide insightful visualizations. Spreadsheet software like Excel or Google Sheets also works well for creating a personalized budget.

Remember, this process is about gaining control of your finances.

It's about creating a clear roadmap for your financial future. By honestly assessing your current situation, you lay the foundation for achieving the financial freedom you deserve. This isn't just about numbers; it's about empowering yourself to take control of your financial life and build the future you envision. The next chapter will delve into specific strategies for tackling debt and creating a robust wealth-building system.

Identifying and Addressing Bad Debt

Now that you've taken stock of your financial landscape – your income, expenses, assets, and liabilities – it's time to address the elephant in the room: bad debt. This isn't just about paying down debt; it's about strategically eliminating the financial anchors holding you back from building wealth. High-interest debt,

particularly credit card debt and payday loans, is a significant obstacle, sucking the life out of your financial progress. These debts often come with exorbitant interest rates, meaning a larger portion of your payment goes towards interest rather than principal,

making it incredibly difficult to pay them off.

Let's tackle this head-on. High-interest debt isn't just a number; it's a psychological burden. The constant worry about minimum

payments, late fees, and the ever-increasing balance can be

crippling. But remember, you're not alone, and you *can* overcome this. Many people have successfully navigated this treacherous terrain and achieved financial freedom. Your journey might be unique, but the principles remain the same.

One common strategy is debt consolidation. This involves

combining multiple debts into a single loan, ideally with a lower interest rate. This simplifies your payments and can save you a substantial amount of money in interest over time. There are several avenues for consolidation:

Balance Transfer Credit Cards: Many credit card companies offer 0% APR introductory periods for balance transfers. This gives you a window of opportunity to pay down a significant chunk of your debt without incurring further interest charges. However, be aware of balance transfer fees (usually a percentage of the transferred amount) and the interest rate that kicks in after the introductory period ends. Carefully plan your repayment strategy to avoid falling behind after the 0% period ends.

Personal Loans: Personal loans can consolidate multiple debts into a single, manageable monthly payment. They often offer lower interest rates than credit cards, speeding up your debt repayment.

Shop around for the best rates and terms, compare offers from banks, credit unions, and online lenders. Consider your credit score, as it will significantly impact the interest rate you qualify for.

Debt Consolidation Loans from Credit Unions: Credit unions are member-owned financial institutions that often offer more

competitive interest rates and flexible terms compared to traditional banks. If you're a member, explore their debt consolidation loan options. They frequently focus on member financial well-being and may offer personalized guidance.

However, debt consolidation isn't always the right solution. It's crucial to carefully assess your overall financial situation before pursuing this route. If you're prone to overspending, consolidating debt into a single, larger loan might lead to additional borrowing.

Once you've consolidated (or decided against it), the focus shifts to repayment strategies. Two popular methods are the debt snowball and the debt avalanche.

The Debt Snowball Method: This focuses on paying off the

smallest debt first, regardless of its interest rate. The psychological satisfaction of quickly eliminating a debt, no matter how small, provides motivation to tackle the larger ones. This method is powerful for building momentum and maintaining morale. Imagine you have four debts: $500, $1,000, $2,000, and $5,000. The

snowball method would start with the $500 debt, then move to the $1,000 debt, and so on.

The Debt Avalanche Method: This method prioritizes debts with the highest interest rates. By focusing on high-interest debts first, you minimize the total amount of interest paid over the life of your loans, saving you money in the long run. Using the same example, the avalanche method would tackle the $5,000 debt first, then the $2,000, and so on. While it may take longer to see early wins, the long-term savings are substantial.

Choose the method that best suits your personality and financial circumstances. The snowball method offers immediate gratification, while the avalanche method offers long-term financial benefits.

There is no right or wrong answer; what matters is that you consistently apply a chosen method and stick to your plan.

Beyond these strategies, negotiating with creditors can be a powerful tool. Many creditors are willing to work with you to avoid losing you as a customer. Here are some strategies for negotiating:

Document Your Financial Situation: Compile a detailed record of your income, expenses, and debts. This demonstrates to creditors your commitment to resolving the situation.

Propose a Written Payment Plan: Offer a realistic repayment plan based on your budget. This shows that you're taking proactive steps to address your debt.

Be Polite and Professional: Maintaining a respectful and professional tone in your communication is essential. Anger or aggression is counterproductive.

Be Prepared to Negotiate: Creditors may not immediately agree to your proposed plan. Be ready to compromise and negotiate a mutually agreeable solution.

Get it in Writing: Once you reach an agreement, obtain written confirmation from the creditor outlining the terms of the plan.

Remember, negotiating takes courage and patience. It's a conversation, not a confrontation. Your goal is to find a solution that works for both you and the creditor. If one creditor isn't willing to work with you, try another.

Let's look at a real-life example. Sarah, a millennial graphic designer, found herself burdened with $10,000 in credit card debt, with interest rates ranging from 18% to 24%. She felt overwhelmed and hopeless. After carefully tracking her expenses and income, Sarah decided to use the debt avalanche method. She prioritized her highest interest debt and created a budget that allowed her to allocate extra funds towards that specific card. She also negotiated with her credit card company, securing a lower interest rate on her highest-interest card. Through disciplined budgeting, and consistent payments, Sarah successfully paid off her credit card debt within 18 months. Her story highlights the power of commitment, strategy, and effective negotiation.

Overcoming debt is a marathon, not a sprint. There will be setbacks and challenges along the way, but remember, progress is progress. Celebrate the small victories, stay focused on your goals, and don't be afraid to ask for help. You've already taken the first critical step by acknowledging your debt and deciding to take control. Now, implement the strategies discussed, track your progress

meticulously, and celebrate each milestone as you move closer to a debt-free future. This journey is yours to conquer. Your financial future is within your reach. The next step is building a robust wealth-building system to ensure you never return to this

precarious position.

Building a Realistic Budget That Works

Now that we've conquered the beast of high-interest debt, let's shift our focus to building a sustainable financial foundation: a realistic budget. Many young adults view budgeting as a restrictive, joyless chore, but I see it as a powerful tool, a roadmap to financial

freedom. It's about consciously choosing how you spend your money, aligning your spending with your values, and ultimately, achieving your financial goals. A well-crafted budget isn't about deprivation; it's about mindful spending and strategic saving, enabling you to live a fulfilling life while building wealth.

Forget the rigid, outdated budgeting methods. We'll explore strategies tailored to the dynamic lives of millennials and Gen Z. We'll discuss methods that empower you to take control of your finances, without feeling like you're constantly sacrificing

everything you enjoy.

One effective approach is **zero-based budgeting (ZBB)** . This method involves allocating every dollar of your income to a specific expense category, ensuring that your income equals your expenses. It requires a detailed look at your spending habits and forces you to prioritize where your money goes. It's not about cutting everything out; it's about making conscious choices about your spending.

To begin, you'll need to meticulously track your expenses for at least a month. Utilize budgeting apps like Mint, YNAB (You Need A Budget), Personal Capital, or even a simple spreadsheet. These tools automatically categorize your transactions, providing a clear picture of where your money is going. The goal isn't to judge your past spending but to understand your spending patterns. Are you

consistently overspending in certain areas? Are there areas where you can easily cut back?

Once you have a clear understanding of your spending habits, create a budget using the zero-based approach. List all your income sources—salary, side hustles, investments—and then meticulously allocate every dollar to a specific expense category. Include everything: rent or mortgage, utilities, groceries, transportation, entertainment, debt payments, savings, and any other expenses. The key is to allocate every single dollar. If you have any money left over at the end, it's an excellent opportunity to allocate it to savings or investments.

While ZBB offers detailed control, the **50/30/20 rule** provides a simpler framework. This rule suggests allocating 50% of your after-tax income to needs, 30% to wants, and 20% to savings and debt repayment. Needs include essential expenses like housing, food, transportation, and healthcare. Wants are non-essential expenses like entertainment, dining out, and shopping. The 20% allocated to savings and debt repayment is crucial for building wealth and securing your financial future.

The beauty of the 50/30/20 rule lies in its simplicity. It provides a guideline, but it's flexible enough to adapt to your unique

circumstances. If you're aggressively paying down debt, you might allocate a larger percentage to debt repayment, potentially reducing the amount you allocate to wants. The key is to find a balance that works for you and your financial goals. Remember, this is a

guideline, not a rigid rule. Experiment, adjust, and find what fits best with your lifestyle.

Regardless of the budgeting method you choose, consistent tracking is paramount. Use the budgeting apps we discussed earlier, or develop your own system using a spreadsheet. Regularly review your budget, compare your actual spending to your planned

spending, and make adjustments as needed. Life throws curveballs; your budget should be flexible enough to handle them. A stagnant budget quickly becomes irrelevant in the face of changing

circumstances.

One common budgeting pitfall is failing to account for irregular expenses. These include car repairs, unexpected medical bills, holiday expenses, or annual insurance payments. It's tempting to ignore these, but a realistic budget must account for them. Create a separate category for irregular expenses, saving a small amount each month to build a cushion. This prevents you from going into debt when unexpected costs arise.

Another crucial aspect of budgeting is tracking your net worth—your assets minus your liabilities. This provides a broader perspective of your financial health. Track your assets (cash, investments, savings, property) and your liabilities (debt, loans). Regularly monitoring your net worth helps you assess your progress towards your financial goals and identify areas needing improvement.

Lastly, remember that budgeting isn't a one-time task; it's an ongoing process. Your financial circumstances will change; your budget should evolve with them. Don't be discouraged if you slip up occasionally. The important thing is to get back on track and continue to refine your budget until it works effectively for you.

Treat your budget as a living document, regularly reviewing and adjusting it based on your current financial situation and goals.

Let's delve into a few practical examples. Imagine you're a recent college graduate earning $40,000 annually after taxes. Using the 50/30/20 rule, your monthly budget might look like this:

50% Needs ($1667): Rent ($1000), Groceries ($300), Utilities ($150), Transportation ($100), Student Loan Payment ($117).

30% Wants ($1000): Entertainment ($300), Dining Out ($200), Clothing ($150), Personal Care ($100), Subscriptions ($250).

20% Savings and Debt Repayment ($667): Emergency Fund ($333), Retirement Savings ($334).

This is merely a sample budget. Your specific allocation will differ based on your income, expenses, and financial goals. Remember, this example includes debt repayment, demonstrating how easily you can integrate debt management into your monthly budgeting.

Now, let's consider a scenario where you're facing unexpected expenses. Perhaps your car needs significant repairs, costing

$1,000. Instead of going into debt, draw upon your emergency fund. If your emergency fund doesn't cover the full cost, reassess your budget for the upcoming month, potentially reducing your "wants" spending to allocate more towards the repairs. By having a solid budget in place, you're prepared to tackle unexpected expenses without jeopardizing your financial stability.

Remember, budgeting is about building a sustainable financial framework, a structure that allows you to live within your means while steadily building wealth. It's about consciously choosing how you spend your money, ensuring it aligns with your values and financial goals. It's not a restrictive regimen; it's an empowering tool that puts you firmly in the driver's seat of your financial life, helping you transition from a position of financial struggle to one of security and eventual freedom. This detailed approach to budgeting forms a critical foundation for the wealth-building strategies we'll cover in subsequent chapters, making sure that your journey to financial success is both sustainable and fulfilling.

Setting SMART Financial Goals

Now that you have a solid understanding of your spending habits and have implemented a budget that works for you, it's time to take the next crucial step: setting SMART financial goals. Many people drift through life financially, reacting to circumstances rather than proactively shaping their future. Setting SMART goals empowers you to take control, defining your financial aspirations and creating a roadmap to achieve them. This isn't about dreaming; it's about planning, strategizing, and relentlessly pursuing your financial objectives.

The acronym SMART stands for Specific, Measurable, Achievable, Relevant, and Time-bound. Each element is critical in crafting goals that are both motivating and attainable. Let's break down each component:

Specific: Vague goals lead to vague results. Instead of saying "I want to save more money," a specific goal would be "I want to save $10,000 for a down payment on a house within the next two years." Notice the clarity. The goal is precisely defined, leaving no room for ambiguity. Similarly, instead of "I want to pay off my debt," a specific goal would be "I want to pay off my $5,000 credit card debt within 12 months." The specificity provides focus and direction. The more detailed your goal, the easier it will be to track your progress and stay motivated.

Measurable: How will you know when you've reached your goal? A measurable goal includes quantifiable metrics. For example,

"Increase my net worth by $20,000 in five years" is measurable. You can track your progress regularly and see how close you are to achieving your target. Conversely, "Improve my financial situation" is not measurable. It lacks concrete metrics to gauge success.

Consider how you will measure your progress. Will you use a spreadsheet, a budgeting app, or a financial tracking software?

Choosing the right tools will significantly aid in tracking and ensuring accountability.

Achievable: While ambitious goals are admirable, they must also be realistic. Setting a goal to become a millionaire overnight is unrealistic for most people. Achievable goals challenge you, but they also remain within the realm of possibility, given your current financial situation and resources. Consider your income, expenses, and time constraints when setting your goals. Break down large goals into smaller, more manageable steps. For instance, the goal of saving $10,000 for a down payment might be broken down into monthly savings targets of $417. This smaller, more achievable step makes the larger goal seem less daunting.

Relevant: Your financial goals should align with your overall life goals and values. If your dream is to travel the world, saving for a down payment on a house might not be the most relevant goal. Ensure your financial goals support your larger life aspirations. For example, if you value financial independence, your goals will

revolve around wealth building and securing your financial future. If you value experiences, your goals might focus on saving for travel and pursuing passions. The relevance of your goals ensures that your financial efforts contribute directly to the life you envision for yourself.

Time-bound: Every goal needs a deadline. This creates urgency and focus. A time-bound goal might be "Pay off my student loans in three years," or "Save $5,000 for a down payment within 18

months." Setting a deadline compels you to take action and stay on track. Without a deadline, goals can easily become procrastination traps, never making the transition from aspiration to reality. Time-bound goals introduce an element of accountability, transforming your dreams into tangible steps with specific timelines.

Let's illustrate the importance of SMART goals with examples.

Poorly Defined Goal: "Get out of debt." This goal is too vague. It lacks specificity, measurability, and a timeline.

SMART Goal: "Pay off my $8,000 credit card debt with a 15% interest rate within 18 months by making minimum payments plus an additional $250 per month." This goal is specific, measurable (you track the balance), achievable (it's realistic based on your budget and repayment strategy), relevant (it aligns with the desire to improve your financial health), and time-bound (18 months).

Poorly Defined Goal: "Save money for retirement." This goal lacks specificity and measurability.

SMART Goal: "Contribute $500 per month to my Roth IRA for the next 30 years to reach a retirement savings goal of $500,000." This goal is specific, measurable (you can monitor your IRA balance), achievable (assuming your budget allows for the monthly contributions), relevant (it aligns with long-term financial security), and time-bound (30 years).

Poorly Defined Goal: "Buy a house." This goal is too broad.

SMART Goal: "Purchase a three-bedroom house in [specific neighborhood] priced between $300,000 and $350,000 within the next three years by saving $1,000 per month for a down payment and obtaining a mortgage pre-approval within six months." This goal is specific (house type, location, price range), measurable (track savings, mortgage application status), achievable (based on your financial situation and market conditions), relevant (it aligns with the desire for homeownership), and time-bound (three years).

Now, let's move beyond examples and delve into the practical application of these principles in your own life. Take some time to reflect on your financial aspirations. What are your short-term and long-term goals? Use the SMART framework to refine these aspirations.

Exercise: List at least three short-term and three long-term financial goals. For each goal, describe how it aligns with your overall life goals and values. Then, rewrite each goal using the SMART framework, ensuring that it is specific, measurable, achievable, relevant, and time-bound.

This exercise is crucial for converting your financial dreams into actionable plans. Remember, achieving your financial goals is not a sprint; it's a marathon. Consistent effort, informed decision-making, and regular progress reviews are key to success. Regularly review your progress, adjust your goals as needed, and celebrate your milestones along the way. The journey to financial freedom is a personal one, shaped by your unique aspirations and circumstances.

But by employing the SMART goal-setting framework, you'll

transform your aspirations into a tangible, achievable path towards financial independence. This structured approach ensures that you're not just dreaming about your financial future; you're actively building it, one SMART goal at a time. The commitment to setting, tracking and achieving these goals will prove to be one of the most powerful tools you will ever use to gain control over your financial future.

Mindset Shift From Broke to Boss

The journey to financial freedom isn't just about numbers on a spreadsheet; it's a deeply personal transformation. It's about shifting your mindset from a place of scarcity and struggle to one of

abundance and empowerment. This is where the real magic

happens. You can have the most meticulously crafted budget, the most sophisticated investment strategy, but without the right

mindset, you'll likely find yourself constantly battling against self-sabotage and falling short of your goals. Think of your mindset as the engine that drives your financial vehicle; without a powerful, well-tuned engine, even the most beautiful car won't get you far.

Many millennials, myself included, started our financial journeys feeling overwhelmed, even defeated. We were bombarded with messages suggesting that financial success was reserved for a select few, that it required some innate talent or stroke of luck. We felt burdened by student loan debt, stagnant wages, and the ever-increasing cost of living. This sense of being trapped, of being perpetually “broke,” can be paralyzing. It breeds inaction,

procrastination, and a feeling of hopelessness. But I'm here to tell you that this is a lie, a limiting belief that holds you back from achieving your full financial potential.

The truth is, financial success is not a lottery; it's a skill you can learn and develop. It's about making conscious choices, taking consistent action, and, most importantly, believing in your ability to succeed. This section is dedicated to helping you cultivate that belief, to help you shift your mindset from "broke" to "boss" of your own financial destiny.

The first step in this transformation is to identify and challenge your limiting beliefs about money. These are the negative, often subconscious, thoughts and assumptions that hold you back from making positive financial decisions. Common limiting beliefs include:

Money is the root of all evil: This belief often stems from a fear of greed or materialism. While excessive materialism can be detrimental, money itself is simply a tool. It's a resource that can be used for good or bad, depending on your intentions and how you manage it. The key is to use it wisely, to align your financial goals with your values, and to avoid becoming a slave to material

possessions.

I'm not good with money: This is a self-fulfilling prophecy. If you believe you're not good with money, you're less likely to engage in the learning and effort required to manage it effectively. The truth is, financial literacy is a skill, not an innate talent. It can be learned and improved upon with consistent effort and the right resources.

I don't have enough money to invest/save: This is a common excuse, particularly for those starting with limited resources.

However, even small amounts can make a difference over time. Begin with what you have; every little bit counts. Consistency, not the size of your initial investment, is key. Consider automating your savings to ensure regularity and prevent impulse spending.

I'll deal with my finances later: Procrastination is the enemy of financial success. The longer you wait to take control of your finances, the more difficult it becomes. Addressing your finances proactively, no matter how overwhelming it might feel initially, is critical for long-term financial well-being.

Once you've identified your limiting beliefs, actively challenge them. Replace negative thoughts with positive affirmations. Instead of saying "I'm bad with money," try "I am learning to manage my finances effectively." Instead of "I'll never be rich," try "I am

creating a plan to achieve my financial goals." This may sound simplistic, but the power of positive self-talk is undeniable.

Building financial confidence requires consistent action and

celebrating your small victories. Each step you take, no matter how small, is a testament to your commitment to improving your

financial situation. Track your progress, acknowledge your

accomplishments, and learn from your mistakes. Don't let setbacks derail you; view them as learning opportunities, adjusting your strategies as needed.

Developing a proactive approach means actively seeking knowledge, taking initiative, and making conscious choices about your money. This includes budgeting, saving, investing, and seeking professional advice when needed. It's about taking control of your financial destiny rather than reacting passively to circumstances.

Maintaining motivation and perseverance requires a multi-pronged approach. First, build a support network. Surround yourself with people who support your goals, who can provide encouragement and accountability. Consider joining online communities or finding a mentor who can guide you on your journey. Second, find ways to stay motivated. Set realistic goals, celebrate your successes, and reward yourself for your hard work. Third, develop strategies for dealing with setbacks. When you encounter obstacles, which you inevitably will, don't let them discourage you. Analyze what went wrong, adjust your strategies, and keep moving forward. Remember that building wealth is a marathon, not a sprint.

Furthermore, incorporating mindfulness and self-compassion into your financial journey is crucial. Mindfulness allows you to observe your thoughts and emotions without judgment, enabling you to recognize and address limiting beliefs and emotional spending patterns. Self-compassion means treating yourself with kindness and understanding, especially during setbacks. Remember that everyone makes mistakes; it's part of the learning process. Instead of beating yourself up over financial errors, acknowledge them, learn from them, and move on.

The transition from a mindset of scarcity to one of abundance isn't instantaneous; it's a gradual process that requires consistent effort and self-reflection. It requires actively challenging negative beliefs, replacing them with empowering affirmations, and consistently practicing positive financial habits. It's about viewing money as a tool to achieve your dreams and goals, not as a source of stress and anxiety. By focusing on your progress, celebrating your achievements, and learning from your mistakes, you'll steadily build the confidence and competence you need to become the"boss" of your own financial future. Remember that this isn't about overnight transformations; it's about cultivating a sustainable, long-term relationship with your finances, a relationship built on empowerment, knowledge, and self-belief. Your financial journey is yours alone, shaped by your unique circumstances and aspirations. Embrace the journey, learn from your experiences, and remember that you are capable of achieving financial success. You have the power to shift your mindset, to take control, and to build the life you've always dreamed of.

Exploring Side Hustle Opportunities

Now that we've laid the groundwork for a powerful financial mindset, let's dive into the practical strategies for building wealth.

A key component of this is diversifying your income streams. Relying solely on a single source of income, especially in today's volatile economic climate, is risky. Building multiple income streams provides a safety net, accelerates your progress towards financial freedom, and offers a greater sense of financial security.

One incredibly effective way to achieve this is by exploring the world of side hustles.

Side hustles, those extra income-generating activities you pursue outside your primary job, are no longer a niche concept but a mainstream strategy embraced by millions. They're accessible, flexible, and offer a powerful way to boost your earnings and build financial resilience. The beauty of a side hustle lies in its ability to leverage your existing skills, passions, or interests, transforming them into a valuable income source. This isn't about working harder; it's about working smarter, finding ways to monetize your talents and create additional income streams without necessarily sacrificing your personal time or existing commitments.

The digital age has exploded the potential of side hustles, offering a diverse range of opportunities that were unimaginable just a few decades ago. Let's explore some of the most prominent and

accessible options:

Freelancing: Turning Your Skills into Dollars

Freelancing is a dynamic and increasingly popular side hustle, allowing you to offer your services to clients on a project-by-project basis. If you possess writing, editing, graphic design, web

development, virtual assistance, or any other marketable skill, you can easily find clients online. Platforms like Upwork, Fiverr, and Freelancer.com connect freelancers with businesses and individuals seeking their expertise.

The key to success in freelancing is to specialize in a specific area where you have demonstrable expertise. Don't try to be a jack-of-all-trades; focus on a niche that allows you to command higher rates and attract a loyal clientele. Building a strong online portfolio showcasing your best work is essential. This portfolio serves as your credibility and allows potential clients to assess your abilities before hiring you. Furthermore, actively networking and building

relationships within your chosen field will significantly increase your chances of landing lucrative projects. Positive reviews and testimonials from satisfied clients are invaluable, boosting your reputation and attracting more work.

Consider Sarah, a millennial graphic designer who worked a full-time job in a marketing agency. Unsatisfied with her salary, she started freelancing on the side, offering logo design and branding services. By meticulously building her portfolio and networking online, she quickly gained a loyal client base. Within a year, her freelance income surpassed her full-time salary, allowing her to eventually leave her corporate job and pursue her entrepreneurial passion full-time. This is a testament to the earning potential of freelancing when approached strategically.

Online Tutoring: Sharing Your Knowledge, Earning Income

If you have expertise in a particular subject, online tutoring can be a highly rewarding side hustle. Platforms like Chegg, TutorMe, and Skooli connect tutors with students needing help in various

academic areas, from elementary school to college level. The flexibility of online tutoring allows you to set your own hours, choose your subjects, and work from anywhere with an internet connection.

The key to success in online tutoring is to be patient, enthusiastic, and possess strong communication skills. Creating engaging and effective lesson plans is essential, ensuring that your students

understand the material and make progress. Positive student

reviews and testimonials are crucial for building your reputation and attracting more clients. Many successful online tutors specialize in a specific subject or age group, allowing them to command higher rates and cater to a niche market. Consider building a

personalized website or utilizing social media platforms to advertise your services and reach a wider audience.

Imagine David, a recent college graduate with a degree in

mathematics. Facing limited job prospects, he turned to online tutoring. Leveraging his strong math skills and engaging teaching style, he rapidly built a thriving business, tutoring students in algebra, calculus, and statistics. His flexible schedule allowed him to supplement his part-time job income while building his

professional reputation and gaining valuable teaching experience.

E-commerce: Building Your Online Empire

E-commerce presents a vast landscape of possibilities for side hustlers. From selling handmade crafts on Etsy to dropshipping products from AliExpress, the opportunities are seemingly endless. The key to success in e-commerce lies in identifying a niche market with high demand and low competition. Thorough market research is crucial to ensure that your products will sell.

Building a strong brand identity is essential, conveying the unique value proposition of your products and building customer loyalty.

Effective marketing strategies, including social media marketing and search engine optimization (SEO), are crucial for driving traffic to your online store. Customer service is paramount, ensuring that your customers have a positive experience and are likely to return for future purchases. Managing inventory, processing orders, and handling shipping logistics efficiently are key operational considerations.

Consider Maria, a millennial with a passion for sustainable fashion. She started an e-commerce store selling handcrafted clothing made from recycled materials. By targeting an environmentally conscious niche market and employing effective marketing strategies, she rapidly grew her business, transforming her passion into a profitable side hustle. Her success underscores the importance of identifying a niche market and building a strong brand identity.

Gig Economy Platforms: Leveraging the Power of Apps

The gig economy has revolutionized the world of side hustles, offering a plethora of opportunities through apps like Uber, Lyft, DoorDash, and Instacart. These platforms connect individuals with immediate, short-term work opportunities, providing flexibility and the ability to earn money on your own schedule. The earning potential varies depending on the platform, location, and time commitment.

Success in the gig economy often hinges on efficiency, reliability, and excellent customer service. Maintaining a high rating on these platforms is essential for attracting more gigs and maximizing your earnings. Understanding the local market and demand patterns can also optimize your earnings. For instance, drivers might focus on peak hours or areas with high demand to maximize their hourly rate.

John, a college student, used ride-sharing and food delivery apps to supplement his tuition costs. By strategically choosing his working hours, he was able to earn enough to significantly reduce his

financial burden. This illustrates the power of the gig economy in providing immediate access to income opportunities.

These are just a few examples of the many side hustle opportunities available in the digital age. The key is to identify an option that aligns with your skills, interests, and available time. Start small, experiment with different approaches, and learn from your

experiences. Remember that consistency and perseverance are crucial for building a successful side hustle. Treat your side hustle as a business, even if it's a small one. Develop a solid business plan, track your income and expenses, and continuously strive to improve your efficiency and effectiveness. The rewards—financial freedom, increased security, and the satisfaction of creating something from nothing—are well worth the effort. Remember, the journey to financial success is a marathon, not a sprint. Embrace the

challenges, learn from your mistakes, and celebrate your successes along the way. You have the power to shape your financial future, one side hustle at a time.

Negotiating Your Salary and Benefits

Now that we've explored the exciting world of side hustles and the diverse avenues for generating multiple income streams, it's crucial to address another critical aspect of financial empowerment: negotiating your salary and benefits. While side hustles provide supplementary income, your primary employment remains a significant source of financial stability and growth. Mastering the art of salary negotiation can significantly impact your long-term financial well-being, placing you on a faster track towards your financial goals.

Many millennials shy away from salary negotiations, feeling uncomfortable or unprepared to advocate for their worth. This hesitancy often stems from a lack of knowledge, confidence, or experience. However, effectively negotiating your compensation package is not about being aggressive or demanding; it's about presenting your value proposition clearly and confidently, showcasing the tangible contributions you bring to the table.

Before stepping into a salary negotiation, thorough research is paramount. Understanding the market value for your role, skills, and experience is crucial. Online resources like Glassdoor,

Salary.com, and Payscale provide valuable salary data based on location, industry, and job title. These platforms allow you to benchmark your current compensation against industry standards, giving you a realistic understanding of your worth.

Beyond online resources, networking plays a pivotal role.

Connecting with colleagues, mentors, and professionals in your field provides invaluable insights into salary ranges and compensation packages. Informal conversations can unearth hidden information and reveal industry norms, painting a more comprehensive picture of what you can reasonably expect. Remember, networking isn't just about seeking jobs; it's about building relationships that provide you with vital information and support.

Once you've conducted your research and established a clear understanding of your market value, it's time to quantify your achievements and contributions. Create a concise yet

comprehensive document highlighting your key accomplishments, quantifying your impact whenever possible. Instead of simply stating that you "improved efficiency," showcase specific numbers: "Improved team efficiency by 15% through the implementation of a new workflow, resulting in a $X cost savings." This approach

transforms abstract claims into tangible evidence of your value.

Next, develop a range of salary expectations, accounting for both your research and your personal aspirations. Don't just focus on a single figure; having a range allows for flexibility during the negotiation process. Your research will serve as the foundation for your lower limit, while your aspirations will inform your upper limit. Remember, it's okay to aim high, provided your request is grounded in evidence and aligns with industry standards. Overly ambitious demands, detached from reality, can harm your chances of a successful negotiation.

When it comes to the actual negotiation, confidence is key.

Practicing your pitch beforehand is essential. Rehearse your key points, anticipated questions, and potential counterarguments.

Consider role-playing with a friend or mentor to build your

confidence and refine your communication style. Remember, a confident demeanor communicates competence and increases your negotiating power.

During the negotiation, maintain a professional and respectful tone.

Focus on the value you bring, emphasizing your skills,

achievements, and potential contributions. Present your salary expectations calmly and confidently, explaining the reasoning behind your request. Avoid getting bogged down in emotional arguments or personal grievances. Focus on the facts and let your accomplishments speak for themselves.

Be prepared for counteroffers. Don't be afraid to ask for time to consider a counteroffer; this demonstrates your thoughtfulness and gives you the opportunity to re-evaluate your position. If a

counteroffer doesn't meet your expectations, don't be afraid to politely push back. Remember that you are not only negotiating salary; you are also negotiating benefits. Health insurance, retirement contributions, paid time off, professional development opportunities – all these components contribute to your overall compensation package.

Negotiating benefits requires the same level of preparation and confidence as negotiating salary. Research industry standards for benefits packages, considering factors like your location, company size, and industry. If a particular benefit is important to you, such as flexible work arrangements or specific health insurance options, be prepared to discuss it openly and respectfully. Remember, benefits are a critical part of your total compensation.

Throughout the negotiation process, maintain open and honest communication. Listen attentively to the employer's perspective and address their concerns. Focus on finding a mutually agreeable solution that acknowledges both your needs and the company's constraints. A successful negotiation is not about winning or losing; it's about achieving a fair and equitable outcome that benefits both parties.

Let's consider a real-life example. Imagine Sarah, a data analyst with three years of experience. Through her research, she

discovered that the average salary for her role in her city was between $65,000 and $75,000. She had consistently exceeded expectations in her previous role, streamlining data processes and increasing efficiency by 20%, resulting in a $50,000 cost savings. She prepared a concise document detailing these accomplishments and practiced her salary negotiation with a friend.

During the interview, she confidently presented her salary

expectations within the $70,000 to $75,000 range, explicitly

referencing her accomplishments and their quantifiable impact. The employer initially offered $68,000, but after a respectful discussion, they agreed to $72,000, recognizing the significant value Sarah brought to their team. This demonstrates the power of preparation, research, and confident communication.

Remember, salary negotiation is a skill that improves with practice. Don't be discouraged if your first negotiation doesn't go exactly as planned. Each experience provides valuable learning opportunities, refining your approach and increasing your confidence for future negotiations. Embrace these experiences, learn from your successes and setbacks, and continue to build your negotiating prowess.

This subsection isn't just about salary; it's about claiming your worth. It's about understanding your market value, developing the confidence to advocate for your needs, and securing the financial foundation that will propel you toward your financial goals. It's a crucial step in securing a strong financial future, one that empowers you to achieve your personal and professional ambitions. By

mastering the art of salary negotiation, you not only enhance your earning potential but also cultivate valuable skills in

communication, self-advocacy, and assertive confidence – assets that extend far beyond the confines of a salary discussion.

Beyond the monetary aspects, the process of negotiating your salary and benefits enhances your overall confidence and self-worth. The act of assertively advocating for your needs is empowering,

fostering a sense of agency and control over your financial destiny. This empowerment extends beyond your financial life, influencing your professional development, personal relationships, and overall well-being.

Finally, remember that the negotiation process isn't solely about the initial offer; it's about the long-term relationship you build with your employer. A successful negotiation establishes a positive dynamic, demonstrating your professionalism and commitment to mutual success. This strong foundation fosters a supportive working environment, promoting career growth and advancement. A fair salary and a comprehensive benefits package are not just rewards; they are investments in your future, solidifying your financial stability and enabling you to pursue your long-term financial

ambitions.

Leveraging Your Skills for Income Generation

Now that we've addressed the importance of negotiating your primary income, let's delve into another powerful strategy for building a robust financial foundation: leveraging your skills for income generation. Many millennials possess a wealth of untapped skills and talents that can be transformed into lucrative income streams. This isn't just about finding a side hustle; it's about

strategically identifying and monetizing your unique abilities to create a diversified income portfolio.

The key lies in recognizing your strengths and passions. What are you truly good at? What activities do you enjoy so much that time seems to fly by? Often, the skills we most naturally possess are the ones that hold the greatest earning potential. Perhaps you're a whiz with computers, a gifted writer, a skilled musician, a passionate cook, or an expert organizer. Whatever your talent, there's likely a market for it.

The first step involves thorough market research. Don't assume there's a demand for your skills; validate your assumptions through research. Start by exploring online platforms like Etsy, Upwork, Fiverr, and Guru. These platforms offer a glimpse into the types of services and products that are in high demand, revealing what skills are valued and how they are being monetized. Pay close attention to the pricing strategies employed by successful freelancers and entrepreneurs. This research not only helps you identify

opportunities but also provides a benchmark for your own pricing.

Consider your network. Who are you connected with? Do your friends, family, and colleagues need services that align with your skills? Networking can unveil hidden opportunities and provide valuable leads. Often, the most rewarding ventures begin with word-of-mouth referrals. Don't underestimate the power of your personal connections in generating initial clients or customers.

Once you've identified a skill you want to monetize and validated market demand, it's time to refine your offering. Consider what specific problems you can solve for your target audience. What unique value do you bring? What differentiates your offering from the competition? Creating a compelling value proposition is crucial for attracting clients and commanding competitive rates.

Let's look at some examples. Imagine you're a skilled graphic designer. Instead of simply offering "graphic design services," you could specialize in creating visually appealing social media content for small businesses. Your value proposition could focus on increasing brand engagement and driving sales through strategically designed visuals. Or, perhaps you're a proficient writer. Instead of offering generic writing services, you might niche down to writing compelling website copy for e-commerce businesses, focusing on optimizing conversion rates.

Another option is to leverage your skills to create and sell digital products. This can be extremely profitable, especially as the demand for online courses, ebooks, templates, and other digital products continues to grow. Think about creating an online course on a topic you're passionate and knowledgeable about. Perhaps you're an expert in project management, financial literacy, or social media marketing. You can package your expertise into a comprehensive online course and sell it through platforms like Teachable, Thinkific, or Udemy.

Similarly, you could compile your knowledge into an ebook or a series of workbooks. If you're skilled in design, you could create and sell templates, such as social media graphics, website banners, or resume templates. The possibilities are virtually limitless, especially in the ever-expanding digital marketplace.

The key is to focus on creating high-quality products that provide genuine value to your target audience. Don't cut corners; invest time and effort in creating a polished product that meets or exceeds customer expectations. Remember, positive reviews and testimonials are invaluable in building trust and credibility.

Furthermore, consider offering different pricing tiers or packages to cater to a wider range of budgets and needs.

Marketing your skills and products is crucial for success. Utilize social media platforms, your personal network, and online marketplaces to reach your target audience. Create a professional website or online portfolio to showcase your work and build credibility. Consider offering a free consultation or sample of your services to attract potential clients. Building a strong online

presence is essential in the digital age.

Let's consider a real-world example. Sarah, our data analyst from the previous section, also possesses excellent communication skills. She noticed that many small businesses struggled with data analysis and reporting. She leveraged her expertise by creating a consulting service, offering personalized data analysis and reporting tailored to the specific needs of small business owners. She marketed her services through her network and social media, emphasizing her ability to translate complex data into actionable insights that helped businesses make informed decisions.

Her success is a testament to the power of identifying and

monetizing a skill that aligns with market demand. She didn't just rely on her primary employment; she actively sought opportunities to leverage her expertise and build additional income streams. Remember, Sarah's journey is not unique; it represents a path many millennials can follow. By thoughtfully identifying and developing their unique skills, they can unlock significant earning potential and pave the way towards financial security and independence.

Beyond generating income, developing and utilizing your skills fosters personal growth and satisfaction. The process of learning new skills, mastering existing ones, and applying them in creative ways is incredibly rewarding. The feeling of accomplishment that comes from building something from the ground up, whether it's a business or a digital product, is inherently fulfilling.

Moreover, this entrepreneurial spirit cultivates self-reliance and independence, empowering you to take control of your financial destiny. It's not just about the money; it's about the satisfaction of using your talents to create value and achieve your financial goals.

This sense of agency is crucial for long-term financial well-being and overall personal fulfillment. By turning your skills into income, you are not only building a robust financial future but also

cultivating a sense of purpose and self-worth. This is the true power of leveraging your skills – a path to financial freedom and personal empowerment. Embrace this journey, explore your potential, and discover the rewarding possibilities that await.

Investing in Your Future Self

Investing in yourself is the most lucrative investment you'll ever make. While generating multiple income streams is crucial for financial stability, it's equally vital to continuously upgrade your skills and knowledge. This isn't just about chasing the next big thing; it's about building a foundation of expertise that will serve you throughout your career and life. Think of it as building compound interest, not just for your bank account, but for your earning potential.

The modern job market is dynamic and competitive. Skills that are in-demand today might be obsolete tomorrow. Staying ahead requires a commitment to lifelong learning – a proactive approach to acquiring new knowledge and refining existing skills. This isn't about simply reacting to market changes; it's about anticipating them and positioning yourself to capitalize on emerging opportunities.

One of the most effective ways to invest in your future self is through formal education. This doesn't necessarily mean going back to university for a four-year degree (though that can be a valuable option for some). Consider pursuing shorter, more focused programs, like vocational certifications, online courses, or boot camps. These programs are often designed to equip you with highly specific, in-demand skills, accelerating your professional development in a shorter timeframe and at a lower cost than a traditional degree.

Many online learning platforms, such as Coursera, edX, Udacity, and Khan Academy, offer a wide range of affordable, high-quality courses in various fields. Some even offer free courses, allowing you to explore new areas of interest without significant financial investment. These platforms often partner with prestigious universities and institutions, ensuring the quality and relevance of the educational content. Look for courses that align with your career goals or address skills gaps in your current profession.

Beyond online courses, consider professional development

workshops and seminars. These focused sessions often provide practical, hands-on training in specific skills, allowing you to apply what you've learned immediately. Many professional organizations and industry associations offer these workshops at reasonable prices, sometimes even providing discounts to members.

Networking opportunities at these events can also be invaluable, expanding your professional connections and uncovering potential career paths.

Networking is another crucial aspect of self-investment. Attend industry events, join professional organizations, and connect with individuals in your field or related areas. These connections can lead to mentorship opportunities, job referrals, and valuable

insights into industry trends. Building a strong professional network isn't just about accumulating contacts; it's about cultivating genuine relationships built on mutual respect and support. Remember, networking is a two-way street – offer assistance to others, share your expertise, and be a valuable member of your professional community.

Mentorship, in particular, offers invaluable guidance and support. Finding a mentor who has achieved success in your chosen field can provide insights and advice that you wouldn't find anywhere else.

They can offer guidance on career progression, help you navigate challenges, and provide crucial feedback on your professional development. Seek out mentors through your network, professional organizations, or online platforms. Remember that building a strong mentor-mentee relationship requires mutual respect, open

communication, and a commitment to personal and professional growth.

Self-directed learning is also a crucial element of this ongoing investment. Embrace a proactive approach to learning by

consistently seeking out new information and resources. Read industry publications, listen to podcasts, and attend webinars to stay up-to-date on the latest trends and advancements in your field.

Developing a habit of continuous learning will not only enhance your skills but will also keep you engaged and motivated in your profession. This proactive approach to learning demonstrates initiative and a commitment to personal and professional excellence, qualities that employers value highly.

Let's consider some examples of individuals who have transformed their career prospects through self-investment. Maria, a marketing assistant with a passion for data analysis, enrolled in an online data analytics boot camp. After completing the program, she landed a data analyst position at a tech startup, significantly increasing her earning potential. Similarly, David, a graphic designer, invested in a series of online courses on user experience (UX) design. This

allowed him to transition into a higher-paying UX design role, demonstrating the potential for career advancement through

targeted skill development.

These are just two examples, but they highlight the

transformational power of self-investment. By proactively seeking opportunities for education and professional development,

individuals can enhance their skills, increase their earning potential, and unlock new career opportunities. Remember, the investment you make in yourself today will yield significant returns in the future, both financially and personally. This is an investment that will continue to pay dividends throughout your career and beyond.

It's a commitment to lifelong learning and continuous growth –essential attributes for navigating a dynamic and competitive job market.

The financial benefits are undeniable. Increased earning potential is the most immediate and obvious return on your investment.

However, the benefits extend far beyond a higher salary. Improved job security, increased career satisfaction, and enhanced

opportunities for advancement are all significant returns on the investment you make in yourself. Consider the long-term

implications: a more fulfilling career, greater financial

independence, and the ability to adapt to the evolving demands of the modern workplace.

Beyond the financial aspects, personal growth and fulfillment are equally important. The process of learning new skills, mastering new challenges, and achieving professional goals is incredibly rewarding. This process builds confidence, resilience, and a sense of accomplishment that extends far beyond the workplace. You'll find yourself more adaptable, resourceful, and capable of tackling new challenges with confidence and competence. This personal growth translates into increased self-esteem, improved mental well-being, and a greater sense of purpose and meaning in your life.

But what if you can't afford extensive training programs? Many resources are available for those on a budget. Government-funded programs, community college courses, and free online resources offer pathways to skill enhancement without significant financial burden. Explore local libraries, which often offer free online

resources and workshops, and look into scholarships and grants that may be available to support your educational pursuits. Remember, even small investments in your skills can yield significant returns over time. Consistency in learning, even in small increments, is more effective than sporadic bursts of intense learning.

The key is to approach this process strategically. Identify skills that align with your career goals and market demands. Prioritize your learning based on the highest impact and potential return on investment. Don't be afraid to experiment with different learning methods and resources to find what works best for you. Remember that the journey of self-improvement is ongoing; it's a commitment to lifelong learning and continuous growth. Embrace this process, and you'll be well-positioned to achieve your professional and financial goals.

Finally, remember that investing in yourself is not a one-time event; it's a continuous process. As the job market evolves, so should your skills and knowledge. Stay informed about emerging trends,

actively seek out new learning opportunities, and adapt your

approach as needed. This commitment to lifelong learning will not only enhance your career prospects but will also contribute to your overall personal and professional fulfillment. By investing in

yourself, you are investing in a brighter, more secure, and more rewarding future. This commitment to ongoing growth and development is the cornerstone of long-term financial success and personal fulfillment. Embrace the journey, and watch your potential blossom.

Creating a Passive Income Portfolio

Building a passive income portfolio is a powerful strategy for securing your financial future. Unlike active income, which requires consistent effort (like your 9-to-5 job), passive income streams generate money with minimal ongoing work. This doesn't mean it's effortless; building these streams requires initial investment of time, money, or both. But once established, they provide a steady flow of funds, bolstering your financial security and providing a crucial safety net. Think of it like planting a financial garden: it takes work to plant the seeds and nurture the growth, but once established, it yields its fruits with less ongoing effort.

One of the most accessible avenues for passive income is dividend investing. Dividend stocks are shares of companies that distribute a portion of their profits to shareholders on a regular basis. These dividends provide a consistent cash flow, and the stock price itself can also appreciate over time, providing potential capital gains.

Before diving in, it's crucial to understand the risks involved. Dividend payments are not guaranteed; companies can reduce or eliminate dividends if their financial performance deteriorates. Therefore, thorough research is essential.

Focus on companies with a history of consistent dividend payments and strong financial stability. Look for companies with a high dividend yield (the annual dividend payment divided by the stock price) but be cautious of exceptionally high yields, as they may signal underlying financial instability. Diversification is key. Don't put all your eggs in one basket. Spread your investments across multiple companies in different sectors to mitigate risk. Consider using a dividend reinvestment plan (DRIP), which automatically reinvests your dividend payments to purchase more shares, allowing your investment to grow exponentially through compounding.

Resources abound to assist your research. Websites like Yahoo Finance, Google Finance, and Bloomberg provide financial data on publicly traded companies, including dividend history and financial statements. Consider consulting with a financial advisor to tailor a dividend investment strategy to your specific financial goals and risk tolerance. Remember, thorough due diligence is critical to mitigating risk in dividend investing.

Real estate investing is another powerful avenue for generating passive income. While purchasing rental properties can be a lucrative option, it requires significant capital and ongoing management responsibilities, including tenant screening, property maintenance, and rent collection. However, the returns can be substantial, particularly in growing markets. A less capital-intensive approach involves Real Estate Investment Trusts (REITs). REITs are companies that own and operate income-producing real estate. They are traded on stock exchanges, making them easily accessible to investors. REITs distribute a significant portion of their income as dividends, providing a consistent passive income stream.

However, REITs are subject to market fluctuations, just like any other stock. Their performance can be affected by economic conditions and changes in the real estate market. Diversification is crucial, even within the REIT sector. Spread your investments across different types of REITs, such as residential, commercial, or industrial, to reduce risk. Research different REITs, focusing on their financial stability, dividend history, and management team. As with dividend stocks, resources like financial news websites and brokerage platforms offer in-depth information on REITs.

The online world presents a wealth of opportunities to create passive income streams. Creating and selling online courses is an increasingly popular method. If you possess expertise in a particular field, you can package your knowledge into an online course and sell it through platforms like Udemy, Teachable, or Thinkific. The initial effort involves creating the course content, but once it's uploaded, it generates passive income with minimal ongoing effort.

Remember that the quality of your course is crucial. It needs to offer significant value to attract and retain students. Effective marketing is also essential to reach your target audience.

Another online approach involves creating and selling digital products. This could be anything from ebooks and templates to stock photos or online design assets. Websites like Etsy, Creative

Market, and Gumroad provide platforms to sell your digital products. The key is to identify a niche market with unmet needs and create high-quality products that address those needs. Again, marketing is crucial to promote your products and reach a wider audience.

Affiliate marketing is another lucrative option. This involves promoting other companies' products or services and earning a commission on sales generated through your unique referral links.

This can be achieved through a blog, social media, or email

marketing. The success of affiliate marketing depends on building a strong audience and establishing credibility and trust with your followers. Choose products or services that align with your

audience's interests and your values.

Licensing your intellectual property is another potential source of passive income. If you've created a unique product, design, or piece of software, you can license its use to others, earning royalties each time it's used. This can be a highly lucrative option, particularly for creative professionals. However, navigating licensing agreements can be complex, requiring legal expertise. Seek professional advice to ensure your intellectual property is adequately protected and your licensing agreements are favorable.

No passive income stream is entirely risk-free. The stock market can fluctuate, real estate values can decline, and online business

ventures can fail. Effective risk management involves

diversification. Spread your investments across multiple income streams to mitigate the risk of a single stream failing.

Diversification reduces the impact of any single loss, ensuring a more stable and consistent overall income flow.

Regularly reviewing and adjusting your passive income portfolio is essential. Market conditions change, new opportunities emerge, and some streams may underperform. Regular monitoring allows you to identify potential problems early and make necessary adjustments.

This might involve reallocating investments, adjusting marketing strategies, or exploring new income streams. A proactive approach to portfolio management ensures your passive income streams remain robust and continue to deliver consistent returns.

Building a passive income portfolio is a journey, not a destination.

It requires dedication, discipline, and a willingness to learn and adapt. However, the rewards are well worth the effort. The

financial security, flexibility, and freedom that passive income provides are invaluable assets in today's dynamic world. By

diversifying your income sources and strategically investing your time and resources, you can create a sustainable financial

foundation, paving the way for a more secure and fulfilling future. Remember to regularly evaluate, refine, and adapt your strategy to maximize its effectiveness and ensure long-term success in your pursuit of financial independence.

Understanding Basic Investment Principles

Understanding the fundamentals of investing can feel daunting, especially when you're bombarded with complex financial jargon. But the truth is, the core principles are surprisingly straightforward. Think of it like learning to ride a bike – it might feel wobbly at first, but with practice and understanding, you'll gain confidence and find it incredibly rewarding. This section aims to demystify

investing, providing a solid foundation for your financial journey.

One of the first things to grasp is your *risk tolerance* . This refers to your comfort level with the possibility of losing money. Everyone's risk tolerance is different. A younger investor with a longer time horizon might be more comfortable with higher-risk investments, like individual stocks, because they have more time to recover from potential losses. Someone closer to retirement, however, might prefer lower-risk investments, like bonds, to protect their principal.

Assessing your risk tolerance is crucial in making investment decisions that align with your personal circumstances and financial goals. Don't feel pressured to invest in something that makes you uncomfortable; a well-defined risk tolerance forms the bedrock of sensible investing.

The concept of *diversification* is equally important. It's the age-old adage of "don't put all your eggs in one basket." Diversification involves spreading your investments across different asset classes, like stocks, bonds, and real estate. This reduces your risk exposure. If one asset class performs poorly, others might offset those losses, cushioning the overall impact on your portfolio. Imagine investing solely in technology stocks. If the tech sector experiences a

downturn, your entire investment could suffer significantly.

However, if you diversify across several sectors—technology,

healthcare, consumer goods, and more—the impact of a single sector's decline will be considerably lessened. Diversification isn't just about different sectors; it's also about geographic diversification (investing in companies in different countries) and asset class

diversification (investing in stocks, bonds, real estate, etc.).

Consider this example: a portfolio containing only tech stocks in the US is significantly riskier than one including stocks from various sectors globally. This is the fundamental principle behind mutual funds and exchange-traded funds (ETFs), which offer instant diversification through a single investment.

Closely related to diversification is *asset allocation* . This is the strategy of dividing your investments across different asset classes based on your risk tolerance and financial goals. A conservative investor might allocate a larger portion of their portfolio to bonds, while a more aggressive investor might favor stocks. The ideal asset allocation can vary greatly depending on individual circumstances, investment timeline, and financial objectives. For example, a young investor aiming for long-term growth might allocate 80% of their portfolio to stocks and 20% to bonds. However, an investor nearing retirement might reverse this allocation to prioritize capital

preservation. Consider consulting with a qualified financial advisor to determine the best asset allocation strategy tailored to your specific needs and risk profile. A professional can help you navigate the complexities of asset allocation and design a personalized investment strategy that aligns with your goals and risk tolerance.

Now, let's explore some basic investment vehicles. *Stocks* represent ownership in a company. When you buy a stock, you become a shareholder and potentially benefit from the company's growth through increased stock value and dividends. *Bonds* , on the other hand, are essentially loans you make to a company or government. You receive regular interest payments and the principal returned at maturity. Both stocks and bonds can be volatile, particularly stocks, but are considered cornerstone investments in most portfolios, offering growth potential and relatively consistent returns

respectively.

Mutual funds pool money from multiple investors to invest in a diversified portfolio of stocks, bonds, or other assets. This is an excellent option for beginners, as it offers instant diversification and professional management at a relatively low cost. *Exchange-traded funds (ETFs)* are similar to mutual funds, but they trade on stock exchanges like individual stocks. They tend to have lower expense ratios than mutual funds and offer greater flexibility in trading.

Both mutual funds and ETFs provide a convenient way to gain exposure to a broad range of assets without needing extensive

investment knowledge.

The power of *compound interest* is another crucial concept to understand. Compounding is the snowball effect of earning interest on your initial investment and also on the accumulated interest. The longer your money is invested, the more significant the impact of compounding becomes. Imagine investing $1,000 annually for 30 years at a 7% annual return. Without compounding, you would simply make $21,000. However, with compounding, the same investment would be worth considerably more after 30 years. It is precisely this compounding principle that highlights the crucial importance of starting to invest early. The earlier you start, the more time your money has to grow, leading to significantly larger returns in the long run. Even small, consistent investments over a long period can accumulate into a substantial sum, thanks to the magic of compounding. Avoid the trap of thinking you need significant amounts to start investing, this isn't true.

Starting early isn't merely a suggestion; it's a strategic imperative. The advantages of early investing are twofold: firstly, the aforementioned power of compounding allows your initial investment to grow exponentially over time, potentially surpassing the accumulated value of larger sums invested later. Secondly, early investment provides you with a significant time buffer to recoup from market fluctuations. Any temporary dips in the market will have less of an impact if you have decades for your investment to recover.

Finally, remember that investing is a long-term game. There will be ups and downs, market fluctuations, and potential short-term losses. Don't panic sell during market downturns. Instead, stay disciplined, stick to your investment plan, and focus on the long-term growth potential. Consider your investment strategy a marathon, not a sprint. Stay informed, regularly review your portfolio, and adapt your approach as your financial circumstances evolve. Consistent effort, informed decision-making, and an understanding of the fundamental principles will pave the way for your long-term

financial success. Investing intelligently and strategically is key to a secure financial future; it's a journey that requires patience,

discipline, and ongoing learning. But by understanding the basic principles outlined here, you'll be well on your way to mastering the art of investing and building a prosperous future.

Investing for Beginners LowCost Index Funds

Now that we've covered the fundamental concepts of investing, let's delve into a practical and accessible entry point for beginners: low-cost index funds. These are often touted as the cornerstone of a successful long-term investment strategy, particularly for those new to the world of finance. Their simplicity and efficiency make them an ideal starting point, allowing you to build a solid financial foundation without getting bogged down in the complexities of individual stock picking or actively managed funds.

So, what exactly are index funds? Imagine the entire stock market as a vast landscape. An index, like the S&P 500, is a carefully selected basket of the largest and most influential companies in that market. An index fund aims to mirror the performance of a specific index. Instead of trying to pick individual winning stocks – a task that requires significant research, expertise, and often luck – an index fund simply invests in all the companies within that index, proportionally to their market weight. This provides immediate diversification, spreading your risk across a wide range of

companies and sectors.

The beauty of index funds lies in their inherent simplicity and low cost. Because they passively track an index, they require minimal management. There's no team of analysts trying to predict market trends or actively trade stocks. This translates directly into lower expense ratios – the fees you pay annually to manage the fund.

These lower costs directly impact your returns, allowing more of your investment to grow over time. Compared to actively managed mutual funds, which often aim to outperform the market (a goal that's notoriously difficult to achieve consistently), index funds offer a cost-effective and efficient way to participate in market growth.

Choosing the right index fund depends on your investment goals and risk tolerance. The S&P 500, mentioned earlier, is a widely popular choice, representing a broad swathe of the US large-cap market.

However, other indices focus on specific market segments, such as small-cap companies (smaller, potentially faster-growing companies), international markets (providing diversification beyond the US), or specific sectors like technology or healthcare. Consider the following points when choosing an index fund:

Investment Goal: Are you saving for retirement, a down payment on a house, or something else? Your time horizon will impact your risk tolerance and the type of index fund suitable for your needs. Long-term investors generally favor higher-equity exposure, while those nearing retirement may prefer a more conservative approach with a higher bond allocation within their chosen index funds.

Risk Tolerance: How comfortable are you with potential fluctuations in your investment value? A lower-risk tolerance might lead you towards broader market indices like the S&P 500, while a higher tolerance might allow for exposure to smaller-cap companies or international markets, which historically have presented greater volatility but also higher potential returns.

Expense Ratio: This is the annual fee charged to manage the fund. Look for funds with expense ratios of 0.1% or less; even small differences in expense ratios can significantly impact your long-term returns. The lower the expense ratio, the better. A simple calculation can highlight this; a fund charging 1% versus 0.1% annually on a $10,000 investment will mean a $90 difference per year. Over several decades, this difference becomes substantial.

Fund Size and History: Larger, more established funds often offer more stability and liquidity. Check the fund's track record and performance history to gain a clearer understanding of its historical volatility and returns. But remember, past performance is not indicative of future results.

Once you've identified a suitable index fund or funds, the next step is to open an investment account. Several online brokerage firms offer user-friendly platforms with low fees, making it easy to buy and sell index funds. Many offer educational resources to further support new investors. Research a few platforms to compare fees, features, and user experience before selecting one. Consider platforms that offer fractional shares; this allows you to invest smaller amounts of money, making index fund investing more accessible, even with limited capital. This is particularly beneficial for those starting their investment journey.

Before making your first investment, remember the importance of carefully considering your budget. Invest only what you can

comfortably afford without compromising your essential expenses or emergency fund. The key here is consistency, not the size of individual contributions. Regular contributions, even small ones, over the long term, harness the power of compounding, making small consistent contributions just as powerful, if not more so, than large infrequent ones.

Making your first investment can be exciting but remember to approach it with a long-term perspective. Avoid emotional reactions to short-term market fluctuations. The key to success with index funds, as with most investments, is discipline and patience. Sticking to your investment plan and resisting the urge to react to market volatility is crucial for long-term growth.

Beyond simply selecting an index fund and investing, ongoing monitoring and adjustments are important. Regularly review your portfolio to ensure it still aligns with your financial goals and risk tolerance. Your circumstances may change over time – you might change jobs, get married, or have children. These life events might necessitate reassessing your investment strategy and making necessary adjustments. Rebalancing your portfolio periodically ensures that your asset allocation remains consistent with your investment plan, a key element for minimizing risk.

Furthermore, consider expanding your knowledge beyond index funds. While they are an excellent starting point, a well-rounded investment strategy might involve exploring other asset classes in the future. This gradual expansion can happen over time as your investment knowledge and experience grow. Continuous learning is key to becoming a more confident and informed investor. Explore reputable financial resources, such as books, articles, and

workshops, to deepen your understanding of financial concepts.

Never stop learning; the financial world is constantly evolving.

In summary, low-cost index funds provide a simple, efficient, and accessible way for beginners to start investing. By carefully considering your investment goals, risk tolerance, and the fund's expense ratio, you can build a solid foundation for long-term

financial success. Remember that investing is a marathon, not a sprint. Patience, discipline, and consistent contributions are crucial to harnessing the power of compounding and achieving your

financial aspirations. Starting small, staying informed, and adapting your strategy as needed will place you firmly on the path toward a secure financial future. Your journey to mastering the art of

investing has just begun, and with the right knowledge and

approach, you're well-equipped to navigate this exciting and

rewarding path. Remember, seeking professional advice from a qualified financial advisor can provide invaluable support and guidance as you embark on this journey. They can help tailor an investment strategy specifically to your needs and circumstances, providing personalized support along the way. Don't hesitate to seek assistance if you require it.

Exploring Different Investment Vehicles

Now that we've established the foundational role of low-cost index funds in building a robust investment portfolio, let's broaden our horizons and explore other investment vehicles that can further enhance your financial strategy. While index funds offer a fantastic starting point due to their simplicity and diversification, a well-rounded approach often incorporates a mix of asset classes to

optimize returns and mitigate risk. This diversification is crucial; it's the financial equivalent of not putting all your eggs in one basket.

One popular alternative to index funds is the Exchange-Traded Fund, or ETF. ETFs are similar to index funds in that they track a specific index or market segment, offering diversification across numerous assets. However, unlike mutual funds, ETFs trade on stock exchanges like individual stocks, providing flexibility in buying and selling throughout the trading day. This liquidity is a key advantage, particularly for investors who need quick access to their funds or wish to react to market shifts more readily than with a mutual fund. Moreover, many ETFs offer specialized exposure to specific sectors, industries, or even geographical regions, allowing for targeted investments beyond the broad market coverage of many index funds. For example, you could invest in an ETF focused solely on technology companies, renewable energy, or emerging markets, potentially tailoring your portfolio to your specific

interests or risk appetite.

However, ETFs also come with their own set of considerations. While generally considered low-cost, the expense ratios of ETFs can still vary significantly, so it's vital to compare different options before making a decision. Furthermore, the commission fees for trading ETFs, while often quite low on many brokerage platforms, should be factored into your overall investment cost. It's important to note that actively trading ETFs to capitalize on short-term market fluctuations can negate the long-term benefits of investing.

Remember, the goal is generally long-term growth, and frequent trading often incurs additional costs and potentially diminishes overall returns.

Another significant asset class to consider is bonds. Unlike stocks, which represent ownership in a company, bonds represent a loan you make to a government or corporation. In return, you receive regular interest payments and the principal repayment at the bond's maturity date. Bonds are generally considered less risky than stocks, offering a more stable income stream. This stability makes them an excellent addition to a diversified portfolio, especially for those nearing retirement or with a lower risk tolerance. However, bond yields – the interest rate earned – are typically lower than the potential returns from stocks, representing a trade-off between risk and reward. The bond market also presents a wide range of choices; government bonds are considered very low risk, while corporate bonds carry varying degrees of risk depending on the financial health of the issuing company.

The diversity within the bond market allows for strategic allocation based on your risk tolerance and investment goals. For instance, you might allocate a portion of your portfolio to government bonds for stability, while a smaller portion could be invested in higher-yielding corporate bonds to enhance overall returns. However, remember that bond prices can fluctuate inversely to interest rates; if interest rates rise, bond prices generally fall, and vice-versa. Understanding this relationship is crucial to managing your bond investments effectively. Diversification within the bond market itself is key; don't concentrate all your bond investments in a single issuer or type of bond.

Real Estate Investment Trusts, or REITs, offer another avenue for diversification. REITs are companies that own or finance income-producing real estate, such as apartments, office buildings, or shopping centers. Investing in REITs provides exposure to the real estate market without the complexities of directly owning and managing properties. REITs typically pay high dividends, making them attractive for investors seeking regular income. However, REITs can be affected by changes in interest rates, economic conditions, and local market trends. Therefore, it's vital to research specific REITs carefully and understand the potential risks before investing. The geographical diversification within your REIT investments is also crucial; investing solely in REITs based in one area or focusing on a single real estate sector (e.g., only residential properties) can leave your investments vulnerable to localized market downturns.

Diversification across these asset classes – index funds, ETFs, bonds, and REITs – is a powerful strategy for mitigating risk. Instead of relying heavily on a single investment vehicle, spreading your investments across multiple asset classes reduces your exposure to potential losses in any one area. For example, if the stock market experiences a downturn, the stability provided by your bond

holdings could help cushion the impact on your overall portfolio.

Similarly, the steady income stream from REITs can offset any losses from other investments. However, diversification isn't just about spreading your investments across different asset classes; it also requires carefully considering your allocation within each class.

Your asset allocation should reflect your individual risk tolerance and investment goals. Younger investors with a longer time horizon may be more comfortable with a higher allocation to stocks and higher-growth investments. In contrast, those nearing retirement often opt for a more conservative approach, with a larger

percentage of their portfolio in bonds and lower-risk investments.

Rebalancing your portfolio periodically is crucial to maintaining your desired asset allocation. Over time, market fluctuations can shift the proportions of your investments. Rebalancing involves selling some of your higher-performing assets and buying some of your underperforming assets, bringing your portfolio back to its target allocation. This systematic approach helps ensure that your investments remain aligned with your risk tolerance and goals.

Remember that all investments carry some degree of risk. There is no such thing as a completely risk-free investment. However, by understanding the inherent risks of different asset classes,

diversifying your portfolio, and rebalancing it periodically, you can significantly reduce your overall risk exposure. It is vital to perform thorough research and consider seeking advice from a qualified financial advisor who can help tailor a diversified investment

strategy specifically to your needs and risk tolerance. They can assist in constructing a portfolio that balances growth potential with risk mitigation, aligning your investments with your long-term financial goals.

Remember that continuous learning is essential for successful investing. The financial landscape is constantly evolving, and staying informed is crucial. Keep exploring different resources; read books, articles, and attend workshops to enhance your

understanding of investment strategies and market trends. A well-informed investor is a more confident and effective investor.

Finally, remember that successful investing is a marathon, not a sprint. Avoid making impulsive decisions based on short-term market fluctuations. Sticking to your long-term investment plan, even during periods of market volatility, is crucial for achieving your financial goals. Patience, discipline, and a commitment to continuous learning are the keys to long-term financial success. Your journey to mastering the art of investing is ongoing; embrace the learning process, adapt your strategy as needed, and stay focused on your long-term financial objectives.

Managing Your Investment Portfolio

Now that we've explored the foundational elements of a diversified investment portfolio, let's delve into the crucial aspect of actively managing it. Building a portfolio is only half the battle; ongoing management ensures its continued growth and aligns with your evolving financial goals and risk tolerance. This involves regular monitoring, strategic adjustments, and a keen awareness of tax implications.

One of the most critical aspects of portfolio management is regular review. How often you review your portfolio depends on your individual circumstances and investment strategy. For many

investors, a quarterly or semi-annual review is sufficient. This review shouldn't just be a passive glance at your account balance; it requires a deeper analysis of your investment performance relative to your benchmarks, such as the S&P 500 index for broad market exposure or sector-specific indices if you've focused on certain areas.

During these reviews, you should assess the performance of each asset class within your portfolio. Are your bond holdings providing the expected level of stability? Are your stock investments

performing in line with or exceeding their projected growth rates?

Are your REITs delivering the consistent dividend income you anticipated? Comparing your actual returns against your projected returns (if you've developed a financial model or used a financial planning tool), enables you to identify areas where your portfolio is exceeding expectations or underperforming.

Understanding the reasons behind any underperformance is equally crucial. Is it due to a broader market downturn, specific sector weakness, or a poor investment choice? Identifying the root cause allows you to make informed decisions about whether to hold onto underperforming assets, adjust your investment strategy, or potentially sell and reinvest elsewhere. Remember, your investment strategy should always be dynamic, adapting to changing market conditions and your personal circumstances.

Rebalancing your portfolio is a key strategy for managing risk and aligning your holdings with your desired asset allocation. Over time, the market's natural fluctuations can cause your portfolio's composition to drift from your initial target allocation. For instance, if you initially aimed for a 60/40 stock-to-bond ratio, strong stock market performance might shift this balance to 70/30. Rebalancing involves selling some of your overperforming assets (in this example, stocks) and reinvesting the proceeds into underperforming assets (bonds) to restore the original 60/40 balance.

The frequency of rebalancing depends on your risk tolerance and investment goals. A more frequent rebalancing (e.g., annually or even semi-annually) is appropriate for investors with a lower risk tolerance, while less frequent rebalancing might be suitable for those with a longer time horizon and higher risk tolerance.

However, even with less frequent rebalancing, regular monitoring remains vital to identify significant deviations from your target allocation.

Tax optimization is another essential component of portfolio management. Understanding the tax implications of your investment choices can significantly impact your overall returns. Different investment vehicles have different tax characteristics. For instance, dividends from stocks and interest from bonds are typically taxed as ordinary income, whereas capital gains from selling investments are taxed at different rates depending on the holding period.

Tax-loss harvesting is a strategy that can help minimize your tax liability. This involves selling investments that have lost value to offset gains from other investments, effectively reducing your taxable income. However, tax-loss harvesting is a complex strategy, and it's important to understand the rules and regulations before implementing it. Seeking professional advice from a qualified financial advisor or tax professional is highly recommended.

Beyond the regular reviews, rebalancing, and tax optimization, proactive management also involves staying informed about current market trends and economic conditions. This necessitates consistent reading of financial news, market analysis, and relevant publications. While it's impossible to perfectly predict market movements, understanding broader trends can help you make more informed decisions and adjust your strategy as needed.

Remember that investment decisions should always be based on your individual financial circumstances, risk tolerance, and long-term goals. What might be a suitable investment for one person could be completely inappropriate for another. For example, a young investor with a long time horizon might tolerate more risk and invest heavily in growth stocks. In contrast, someone nearing retirement would likely favor a more conservative approach, focusing on preserving capital and generating income.

The importance of seeking professional advice cannot be overstated.

A qualified financial advisor can provide personalized guidance tailored to your specific needs and circumstances. They can help you develop an investment plan that aligns with your goals, assists in selecting appropriate investment vehicles, and provides ongoing support as your financial situation evolves. While independent research is valuable, a financial advisor can offer a comprehensive perspective and objective advice, which is especially helpful during periods of market uncertainty. Furthermore, they can provide valuable insights into areas you might not have expertise in, such as tax planning and estate planning.

Investing successfully is a long-term process, not a quick fix. It's a journey of continuous learning, adaptation, and strategic decision-making. It's not merely about accumulating wealth; it's about building a secure financial future that allows you to achieve your personal and financial goals. Embrace the learning process, stay informed, adapt your strategies as needed, and seek professional guidance when necessary. Remember, your financial well-being is an ongoing commitment, and consistent effort and discipline are vital to long-term success. Your portfolio is a reflection of your financial aspirations; manage it effectively, and watch it grow to support the life you envision.

Avoiding Common Investment Mistakes

Now that we've laid the groundwork for building and managing a diversified investment portfolio, let's address the elephant in the room: the common mistakes that can derail even the most well-intentioned investment strategies. Avoiding these pitfalls is crucial for long-term success, and understanding them is the first step towards building lasting financial security.

One of the most significant obstacles to successful investing is emotional decision-making. Our inherent biases, fears, and hopes often cloud our judgment, leading us to make irrational choices that contradict our long-term goals. The classic example is panic selling during market downturns. When the market experiences a sharp correction, fear can grip investors, prompting them to sell their assets at a loss, locking in their losses and missing out on potential future gains. Conversely, the euphoria of a bull market can lead to overconfidence and excessive risk-taking, potentially leading to significant losses when the market inevitably corrects.

Imagine this scenario: You invested in a promising tech startup, and initially, the stock price soared, exceeding all expectations. The thrill of the quick gains might tempt you to invest even more, potentially exceeding your risk tolerance and diversifying away from safer asset classes. However, when the market corrects or the company experiences setbacks, the initial excitement transforms into fear and regret. This emotional rollercoaster can lead to

impulsive decisions, potentially jeopardizing your overall

investment portfolio. Remember, successful investing requires emotional discipline; detachment from short-term market

fluctuations is key to navigating the long-term game.

Another common mistake is chasing trends. The allure of quick riches often leads investors to jump on the bandwagon of the latest hot investment, only to find themselves left holding the bag when the trend fades. This reactive approach often neglects fundamental analysis, focusing instead on hype and speculation. Examples abound: the dot-com bubble of the late 1990s and the

cryptocurrency craze of the early 2010s are prime examples of how chasing trends can lead to devastating losses. While some trendy investments might indeed generate significant returns, they often carry a higher degree of risk.

Instead of chasing the next big thing, focus on understanding the fundamentals of your investment choices. Research the company's financials, its competitive landscape, its management team, and its long-term prospects. A well-researched investment, even if it's not the flashiest or trendiest, is more likely to provide stable, long-term returns than a speculative gamble on a fleeting trend. A classic example of this would be missing out on long-term growth in

companies like Apple or Google early on in their development while chasing the next "hot" tech stock that offered no real sustainable growth.

Neglecting diversification is another widespread error. Putting all your eggs in one basket, whether it's a single stock, a particular sector, or a specific asset class, exposes you to significant risk. Even the most promising investments can fail, and a diversified portfolio mitigates the impact of such setbacks. A well-diversified portfolio includes a mix of asset classes, such as stocks, bonds, real estate, and potentially alternative investments, each with different risk-return profiles. This also includes considering geographical

diversification, spreading your investments across different

countries and economies to reduce the impact of localized events.

Within each asset class, diversification should also extend to individual securities. For example, within the stock market, a diversified portfolio should not be concentrated in a single sector (e.g., technology) or even a handful of companies.

Consider this example: an investor heavily invested in a single energy company, whose performance was initially exceptionally strong. However, a sudden shift in government regulations or a drop in oil prices could significantly impact their investment. The investor, whose portfolio is largely concentrated in a single stock, suffers a major loss.

On the other hand, an investor with a more diversified portfolio, holding investments across different sectors and asset classes, is likely to experience a much less dramatic impact from this single event. The diversified portfolio might still experience some downturn, but the losses are spread out across multiple investments, mitigating the overall impact on their net worth.

Another significant mistake is failing to regularly review and rebalance your portfolio. As market conditions change, so too should your investment strategy. A portfolio that was once well-diversified might become unbalanced over time due to market fluctuations. Regular reviews (quarterly or semi-annually, for example) allow you to assess your portfolio's performance, identify areas of underperformance, and make necessary adjustments to maintain your desired asset allocation. Rebalancing involves selling some overperforming assets and reinvesting the proceeds into underperforming ones, to restore the target balance. This disciplined approach helps manage risk and maintain alignment with your investment goals.

Imagine a portfolio initially allocated 60% to stocks and 40% to bonds. A strong bull market could see the stock allocation rise to 70%, exceeding the initial risk tolerance and leaving the portfolio exposed to a greater market downturn. Rebalancing, in this scenario, would involve selling some stocks and buying bonds to restore the desired 60/40 ratio. This strategy ensures the portfolio doesn't become overly concentrated in one area, mitigating potential risks associated with market shifts.

Ignoring fees and expenses is another frequent oversight. High fees can significantly erode investment returns over time. Before investing in any fund or product, carefully examine the expense ratio, management fees, and any other associated costs. Many investors fail to pay attention to these details, unknowingly surrendering a substantial portion of their returns to fees. The seemingly small difference in expense ratios between two similar funds can compound significantly over time, leading to a substantial difference in overall returns. Choosing low-cost index funds and ETFs can significantly enhance long-term returns.

Let's consider a simple comparison: Two funds both aim to track the S&P 500 index, yet one has an expense ratio of 0.1% while the other has an expense ratio of 1%. Over a 20-year period, this

seemingly small difference translates into a significant reduction in your final return, potentially thousands of dollars. This difference emphasizes the importance of thoroughly comparing fees and expenses before making investment choices.

Finally, a crucial yet often overlooked aspect is the lack of a clear investment plan. Many investors jump into the market without a defined strategy, a defined risk tolerance, or clear investment goals. Investing should not be a random act; it requires careful planning and consideration of your personal circumstances, financial goals, and risk tolerance. A well-defined investment plan provides a roadmap, guiding your decisions and helping you stay focused on your long-term objectives. This plan should also include provisions for regularly reviewing and adjusting the plan as needed to keep pace with your financial goals and market conditions.

In summary, avoiding common investment mistakes requires a disciplined, proactive approach. By understanding your own biases, researching investment opportunities thoroughly, diversifying your portfolio, regularly reviewing and rebalancing your assets,

minimizing fees, and developing a well-defined investment plan, you can significantly improve your chances of achieving long-term financial success. Remember, investing is a marathon, not a sprint, and consistent effort and mindful decision-making are crucial for achieving your financial goals. Your financial future is an

investment in yourself; make it a priority.

Planning for Retirement

Now that we've explored the crucial aspects of building a robust and diversified investment portfolio and the common pitfalls to avoid, let's shift our focus to a critical component of long-term financial security: retirement planning. Securing your financial future beyond your working years requires a proactive and strategic approach, starting well in advance of your retirement date.

Delaying retirement planning often leads to a steeper climb later, making it significantly more challenging to achieve your desired retirement lifestyle.

The cornerstone of successful retirement planning is understanding the various savings vehicles available. One of the most common is the 401(k) plan, a tax-advantaged retirement savings plan

sponsored by many employers. Contributions are made pre-tax, reducing your current taxable income, and the earnings grow tax-deferred until withdrawal in retirement. Many employers offer matching contributions, essentially providing free money towards your retirement savings. Taking full advantage of employer

matching is a crucial step; it's essentially free money, boosting your retirement savings significantly. For example, if your employer matches 50% of your contributions up to 6% of your salary, and you contribute 6%, you're essentially getting a 3% boost to your retirement savings completely free of charge.

However, the benefits of a 401(k) aren't limited to employer

matching. The pre-tax contributions significantly lower your current tax burden, meaning you'll have more disposable income in the present while simultaneously building your retirement nest egg.

Remember to understand the investment options available within your 401(k) plan. Many plans offer a variety of mutual funds, allowing you to diversify your investments across different asset classes and risk levels. Choosing the right mix of investments is key to achieving your long-term retirement goals, aligning with your risk tolerance and time horizon.

Beyond 401(k)s, Individual Retirement Accounts (IRAs) provide another powerful tool for retirement savings. Traditional IRAs, much like 401(k)s, offer tax-deductible contributions, allowing you to reduce your current taxable income. The earnings grow tax-deferred, and withdrawals in retirement are taxed as ordinary income. Roth IRAs, conversely, offer tax-free withdrawals in

retirement. Contributions are made after-tax, but the growth and withdrawals are tax-free, providing a significant advantage in the long run. The choice between a traditional and Roth IRA depends on your individual circumstances, particularly your current and projected tax bracket. If you anticipate being in a higher tax bracket in retirement, a Roth IRA might be more advantageous, while a traditional IRA might be preferable if you expect to be in a lower tax bracket in retirement.

Understanding the contribution limits for both 401(k)s and IRAs is also essential. These limits are adjusted annually to account for inflation, so it's important to stay informed about the most current limits. Contributing the maximum allowable amount each year maximizes your tax advantages and accelerates your savings growth. Remember, the power of compounding works best when you maximize your contributions early on.

But retirement planning extends beyond 401(k)s and IRAs. Consider exploring other tax-advantaged savings plans, such as Health

Savings Accounts (HSAs) if you have a high-deductible health plan.

HSAs allow you to save pre-tax dollars for qualified medical

expenses, offering a triple tax advantage: tax-deductible

contributions, tax-deferred growth, and tax-free withdrawals for medical expenses. While primarily designed for healthcare costs, if you carefully manage your health expenses, you can also treat the HSA as a long-term savings vehicle, with withdrawals allowed for retirement after age 65.

Once you've established a solid foundation with retirement

accounts, it's vital to develop a comprehensive retirement plan. This plan should detail your retirement goals, including your desired lifestyle, estimated expenses, and the timeline for retirement. Based on these factors, you can calculate your required retirement savings, taking inflation into account. Remember that your retirement needs will likely increase over time, and this needs to be factored into your long-term plan. Online calculators and financial advisors can prove helpful in these calculations. Regularly reviewing and adjusting your plan is also essential to account for changes in your circumstances, market conditions, and investment performance.

The timing of your retirement also plays a crucial role in your planning strategy. While many people envision a specific retirement age, your actual retirement might vary based on several factors, including your health, job satisfaction, and financial security.

Delaying retirement, even by a year or two, can substantially

increase your retirement savings due to continued contributions and investment growth. Consider adjusting your retirement timeline based on your financial progress and unforeseen circumstances.

Let's not forget the impact of inflation on your retirement planning. Inflation erodes the purchasing power of money over time. Your retirement savings need to keep pace with inflation to maintain your desired living standards. Factor inflation into your retirement projections to ensure your savings are sufficient to cover your anticipated expenses in future years. Conservative estimates of inflation should be integrated into your financial models.

Furthermore, healthcare costs represent a significant expenditure in retirement. Develop a separate financial plan for healthcare

expenses, taking into account both routine care and potential major medical events. Medicare coverage only covers a portion of

healthcare expenses, and supplemental insurance or savings

specifically allocated for healthcare are crucial to mitigate potential financial burdens. Understanding your healthcare coverage,

including potential gaps in Medicare coverage, and actively

planning for these costs is essential.

Finally, consider diversifying your retirement income streams.

Relying solely on your retirement savings can be risky. Explore additional sources of income, such as part-time work, rental

properties, or investments that provide regular income. This diversification ensures a safety net in case your primary retirement savings fall short of expectations.

Retirement planning isn't a one-time task; it's an ongoing process that requires regular review and adjustment. Your financial circumstances, investment performance, and personal goals are all subject to change. Regularly evaluating your progress, making necessary adjustments to your investment strategy, and ensuring your plan aligns with your evolving needs is crucial for achieving a secure and fulfilling retirement. Staying informed about tax laws, investment options, and retirement planning strategies is also essential to maximizing your retirement savings. Financial advisors can assist you in this process, providing personalized guidance and expert advice. But, ultimately, taking control of your financial future and actively participating in planning your retirement is the most vital step towards achieving your goals. Your retirement is an investment in your future self; make it count.

Protecting Yourself with Insurance

Now that we've laid the groundwork for securing your financial future through strategic investment and retirement planning, let's turn our attention to another crucial pillar of long-term financial security: insurance. Think of insurance as your financial safety net, a crucial buffer against the unexpected life events that can wreak havoc on even the most meticulously crafted financial plan. While no one wants to think about the possibility of accidents, illnesses, or unforeseen circumstances, failing to adequately protect yourself with appropriate insurance coverage can lead to devastating

financial consequences.

Let's start with health insurance, a cornerstone of financial stability, especially in a healthcare system as complex and expensive as the one we have in the United States. The cost of even a minor medical emergency can quickly spiral out of control, potentially leading to crippling debt. Comprehensive health insurance is essential to protect yourself from the financial burden of medical bills, hospital stays, surgeries, and ongoing treatment. Beyond the obvious

medical costs, consider the potential loss of income if you are unable to work due to illness or injury. A robust health insurance plan minimizes these financial risks, allowing you to focus on your recovery rather than worrying about mounting medical debt.

Choosing the right health insurance plan requires careful

consideration of several factors. Understand the different plan types, including HMOs (Health Maintenance Organizations), PPOs (Preferred Provider Organizations), and POS (Point of Service) plans. Each plan type offers a different balance of cost, coverage, and choice of doctors and healthcare facilities. Analyze your needs and healthcare utilization habits to select the plan that best aligns with your budget and healthcare preferences. Don't hesitate to reach out to your employer's human resources department for assistance in understanding your options if you receive benefits through your work.

If you are purchasing health insurance on the individual market, the HealthCare.gov website provides a helpful platform to compare plans and make informed decisions.

Beyond the basic plan features, look carefully at deductibles, co-pays, and out-of-pocket maximums. The deductible is the amount you must pay out-of-pocket before your insurance coverage begins. Co-pays are the fixed fees you pay at the time of a doctor's visit or other healthcare service. The out-of-pocket maximum is the most you will pay in a year for covered healthcare services.

Understanding these key terms is crucial to selecting a plan that fits your budget and reduces the risk of high out-of-pocket medical expenses. Remember, preventive care, such as annual checkups and vaccinations, is often covered at little to no cost, and proactive healthcare can prevent more serious and expensive medical issues in the future.

Next, let's discuss disability insurance, often overlooked but equally critical to protecting your financial well-being. Disability insurance provides income replacement if you become unable to work due to an illness or injury. The possibility of long-term disability is a reality that many people face, and the financial consequences can be severe. Without disability insurance, you could quickly deplete your savings while struggling to meet your financial obligations. Consider short-term disability insurance, covering a shorter period of time, or long-term disability insurance, providing coverage for extended periods. The type of coverage you choose depends on your individual circumstances and risk tolerance. Many employers offer disability insurance as part of their employee benefit packages.

Review these options carefully and consider supplementing your employer's coverage with additional individual coverage to ensure adequate protection.

Life insurance is another crucial aspect of financial planning,

providing financial security for your loved ones in the event of your untimely death. The financial burden of a sudden loss of income can be devastating for surviving family members. Life insurance mitigates this burden, providing a lump sum payment to your beneficiaries, allowing them to cover expenses such as mortgages, debts, education costs, and daily living expenses. Consider term life insurance, providing coverage for a specific period, or whole life insurance, offering lifelong coverage. The type of policy you choose depends on your financial goals and the needs of your loved ones.

Don't underestimate the emotional and financial support life insurance provides, and remember, protecting those you care for is a cornerstone of responsible financial planning.

Homeowners or renters insurance is essential to protect your

property and personal belongings from unforeseen events. For homeowners, this insurance covers damage to your home from various causes, such as fire, theft, or natural disasters. It also

provides liability protection if someone is injured on your property. Renters insurance, similarly, protects your personal belongings from damage or theft and provides liability coverage. Consider the value of your possessions and choose a policy with adequate coverage to replace those items in the event of damage or loss. The relatively small cost of insurance far outweighs the financial devastation of losing your belongings without adequate coverage. Remember to review your policy regularly and adjust the coverage as needed to reflect any changes in the value of your possessions.

Finally, let's not forget about umbrella insurance, often an

overlooked but powerful tool in protecting your finances from potential lawsuits. Umbrella insurance provides additional liability coverage beyond what is provided by your homeowners or auto insurance policies. In today's litigious society, a single accident can lead to significant legal and financial liabilities. Umbrella insurance provides a safety net to protect your assets in the event of a major lawsuit. Consider the peace of mind that umbrella insurance

provides and the protection it offers against potentially devastating financial consequences.

Remember, insurance isn't about preparing for the worst; it's about mitigating the financial impact of the unexpected. It's about

ensuring that life's surprises, however unpleasant, don't derail your long-term financial goals. Regularly reviewing and adjusting your insurance coverage is just as crucial as planning for retirement or investments. Your needs and circumstances change over time, and your insurance needs should reflect those changes. Don't hesitate to seek professional advice from an independent insurance agent to ensure you have the right coverage at the right price. Protecting yourself through comprehensive insurance is an essential

investment in your financial future, providing a critical safety net in an unpredictable world. Think of it as a form of self-care for your financial well-being, a reassurance that no matter what the future holds, you have a plan in place to navigate the unexpected

challenges. Building a secure financial future isn't just about making smart investments and saving diligently; it's also about protecting the fruits of your labor through comprehensive insurance coverage. This is about safeguarding your hard work and providing peace of mind in the face of uncertainty. A proactive approach to insurance is an investment in your future self, a future where unexpected events don't lead to irreparable financial damage.

Estate Planning Basics

Now that we've established the importance of insurance in safeguarding your financial future, let's shift our focus to another critical component of long-term financial security: estate planning. While it might seem like a topic best addressed later in life, estate planning is actually a crucial aspect of financial wellness that's relevant regardless of your age or net worth. Proactive estate planning isn't just about preserving your assets; it's about ensuring your wishes are honored and your loved ones are protected. Think of it as a roadmap for your legacy, guiding how your assets are managed and distributed after you're gone.

The cornerstone of any estate plan is a will. A will is a legal document that outlines how you want your assets – your house, car, savings, investments, and other possessions – to be distributed after your death. Without a will, your assets are distributed according to the laws of your state, a process known as intestacy. This can lead to unintended consequences, potentially leaving your loved ones in a difficult situation, facing legal battles and delays in accessing the funds they need. A will empowers you to make your wishes known, ensuring your assets are distributed according to your intentions.

This could mean leaving everything to your spouse, splitting it between your children, or establishing charitable donations. A well-drafted will also allows you to name a guardian for minor children, ensuring their well-being is prioritized.

Drafting a will is a straightforward process, but it's crucial to seek professional legal advice from an estate planning attorney. While you can find DIY will kits online, these often fall short when dealing with complex situations involving blended families, significant assets, or business ownership. An attorney can help you navigate the legal complexities, ensure your will is legally sound, and that it truly reflects your intentions. They will guide you through the process, asking clarifying questions to make certain you have addressed all aspects of your wishes. A lawyer's expertise can save your loved ones from potential legal challenges down the line. Consider it an investment in peace of mind, ensuring a smooth and efficient transfer of your assets.

Beyond a will, consider establishing a trust. A trust is a legal entity that holds and manages assets for the benefit of another person or group of people. Trusts offer numerous advantages, providing greater control over how and when your assets are distributed. There are different types of trusts, each designed to achieve specific goals. A revocable living trust allows you to maintain control over your assets during your lifetime and allows for modifications as your circumstances change. This can be particularly beneficial for those who wish to avoid probate, the legal process of validating a will and distributing assets, which can be time-consuming and expensive. An irrevocable trust, on the other hand, provides more asset protection and can be used for tax planning purposes. The choice between a revocable or irrevocable trust depends on your specific needs and financial situation, and an attorney can provide valuable guidance in this decision.

The advantages of trusts are significant. They can streamline the distribution of assets, reducing delays and potential conflicts among beneficiaries. They can also offer protection from creditors and lawsuits. Depending on the type of trust, they can facilitate estate tax planning and minimize tax liabilities. In cases involving

complex family dynamics or significant wealth, establishing a trust is a strategy that provides a robust and efficient mechanism for transferring assets. It's a powerful tool that deserves careful

consideration in your estate plan. Again, it is strongly advised to seek professional legal guidance in determining the most suitable trust for your individual circumstances. Navigating the intricate world of trusts requires expertise that only a qualified attorney can provide.

Another essential component of estate planning is a power of

attorney. A power of attorney is a legal document authorizing someone else to make financial and/or healthcare decisions on your behalf if you become incapacitated or unable to manage your affairs yourself. This is crucial to protect your interests and ensure your well-being in the event of unforeseen circumstances, such as a serious illness or accident. A durable power of attorney remains in effect even if you become incapacitated, offering continuous management of your finances and healthcare decisions. A healthcare power of attorney, also known as a medical power of attorney or advance directive, specifically addresses healthcare decisions. This document allows you to name someone you trust to make decisions about your medical care if you are unable to do so yourself.

Choosing the right individuals to serve as your power of attorney is a significant responsibility. Select people you trust implicitly, who understand your wishes and will act in your best interest. Make sure they are reliable, organized, and capable of handling the

responsibilities involved. Communicating your wishes clearly to them is also crucial to ensure a smooth and efficient process. It's recommended to review your power of attorney documents

regularly, updating them as your circumstances change or as you re-evaluate the individuals you've appointed. These documents provide a vital safety net, protecting your interests and ensuring your well-being, even if unforeseen events occur. Do not

underestimate the value of having a properly executed power of attorney in place. It offers peace of mind, knowing that your affairs will be managed effectively should the need arise.

Finally, let's talk about the importance of professional advice. While this chapter provides a basic understanding of estate planning, it is by no means a substitute for professional guidance. The intricacies of estate law are complex and vary significantly depending on your state and individual circumstances. Seeking the advice of an

experienced estate planning attorney is not just recommended; it's crucial. A lawyer will help you navigate the legal landscape, create a comprehensive estate plan tailored to your specific needs, and ensure your wishes are legally protected. They can help you avoid common pitfalls, optimize your plan for tax efficiency, and

minimize the potential for family disputes. Consider the cost of legal advice as an investment in protecting your assets and your legacy. It's an investment that provides peace of mind and ensures that your wishes are honored, and your loved ones are protected. A professional's expertise ensures that your estate plan functions smoothly, minimizing stress for your family during a challenging time.

In conclusion, estate planning is a proactive measure, allowing you to take control of your financial future and provide for your loved ones. It's a vital element of long-term financial security. It's not something to be put off until "later," but a critical step to take as early as possible, ensuring your wishes are respected and your loved ones are cared for. By combining sound financial planning with a comprehensive estate plan, you are building a legacy of financial security for yourself and those you care about. This ensures not only your financial stability but also your peace of mind, knowing that you've taken the necessary steps to protect your future and the future of your family. Remember, seeking professional legal

guidance is a crucial step in this process. Don't hesitate to consult an estate planning attorney to ensure your estate plan is tailored to your unique circumstances and effectively safeguards your legacy.

It's an investment in your future and the future of those you love.

Emergency Fund Strategies

Now that we've explored the crucial aspects of estate planning, let's turn our attention to another cornerstone of long-term financial security: the emergency fund. Think of your emergency fund as your financial safety net, a crucial buffer against unexpected life events. It's the bedrock upon which you build a stable financial future, providing a sense of security and control amidst life's

inevitable curveballs. Without a robust emergency fund, even minor unexpected expenses can quickly spiral into significant financial stress, potentially jeopardizing your long-term goals.

The importance of an emergency fund cannot be overstated. It's not just about avoiding debt; it's about maintaining financial stability and peace of mind. Imagine facing an unexpected car repair, a medical emergency, or a job loss without a financial cushion. The anxiety and potential financial strain can be overwhelming. An emergency fund provides a crucial lifeline, allowing you to navigate these challenges without resorting to high-interest debt or

compromising your long-term financial plans.

So, how much should you save in your emergency fund? A

commonly recommended target is three to six months' worth of living expenses. This ensures you have sufficient funds to cover essential costs, such as rent or mortgage payments, groceries, utilities, and transportation, in the event of an unexpected job loss or other significant financial setback. However, the ideal amount can vary depending on your individual circumstances. Factors such as your job security, your industry, your level of debt, and your personal risk tolerance all influence the appropriate size of your emergency fund. If you have a stable job in a recession-proof industry, you may feel comfortable with a smaller fund, perhaps three months' worth of expenses. Conversely, if you work in a more volatile industry or have higher levels of debt, aiming for six

months or even more may be a wiser approach.

Building your emergency fund might seem daunting, especially if you're starting with little to no savings. But remember, every small step counts. Start by setting a realistic savings goal and breaking it down into smaller, manageable chunks. Set aside a specific amount each month, no matter how small it seems. Even saving $25 or $50 a week adds up over time. Consistent contributions are more important than the size of individual contributions. The key is to establish a consistent savings habit that allows your emergency fund to grow steadily.

There are several effective strategies you can employ to boost your emergency fund savings. One effective technique is to automate your savings. Most banks and financial institutions offer automatic transfer services, allowing you to set up recurring transfers from your checking account to your savings account. This ensures that a predetermined amount is automatically saved each month, making the process effortless and consistent. You'll hardly notice the money leaving your checking account, yet you'll be steadily building your emergency fund. This is a powerful method for building wealth and achieving financial goals because it leverages the power of

consistent, small contributions over time, reducing the need for constant willpower.

Another effective strategy is to identify areas where you can cut back on spending. Review your monthly expenses and identify areas where you can reduce unnecessary spending. This might involve canceling subscriptions you no longer use, reducing dining out expenses, or finding more affordable options for groceries and entertainment. Every dollar saved can be directed toward your emergency fund, accelerating your progress toward your savings goal. Consider using budgeting apps or spreadsheets to track your spending and identify areas for potential savings. These tools can provide valuable insights into your spending habits, helping you make informed decisions about where to allocate your resources.

Staying motivated is crucial when building an emergency fund. It's easy to lose sight of your long-term goal, especially when faced with immediate spending needs. Therefore, find ways to stay motivated. One approach is to visualize the benefits of having a robust emergency fund. Imagine the peace of mind that comes with knowing you have a financial safety net in place, ready to handle unexpected expenses. Visualize how this security will reduce stress and anxiety. Consider setting up a visual reminder, such as a chart tracking your progress towards your savings goal. Seeing your progress visually can provide a significant boost in motivation, reinforcing your commitment to building your emergency fund.

Celebrate your milestones along the way; acknowledge your

achievements and reward yourself appropriately for reaching your savings targets. This positive reinforcement can help you stay focused and motivated, strengthening your commitment to reaching your financial goals.

Consider creating a dedicated savings account specifically for your emergency fund. This separates your emergency funds from your day-to-day spending, making it less tempting to dip into these funds for non-emergency expenses. Keep this account easily accessible, yet discourage unnecessary withdrawals. Many institutions offer high-yield savings accounts that offer a competitive interest rate, allowing your savings to grow slightly faster. Explore these options to maximize your returns, as even small gains contribute to your long-term financial stability.

Don't underestimate the power of small, incremental changes. Every reduction in spending, every automatic transfer, every conscious decision to save contributes to the growth of your emergency fund. Remember, the goal isn't necessarily to achieve the full six months' worth of savings overnight, but to create a sustainable saving habit that will continue to serve you for years to come. Consistency and discipline are key to building a robust emergency fund, providing the financial security you need to weather life's unpredictable storms.

Real-life scenarios can vividly illustrate the importance of an emergency fund. Imagine losing your job unexpectedly. Without an emergency fund, you'd be facing immediate financial pressure, scrambling to pay rent, cover utilities, and feed your family. The stress of this situation could be overwhelming, potentially

impacting your mental and physical health. Having an emergency fund provides a vital lifeline, giving you time to search for a new job without the immediate pressure of mounting debt. It lets you focus on securing your future instead of worrying about immediate survival.

Similarly, consider the scenario of a sudden medical emergency. Medical bills can quickly accumulate, potentially leading to crippling debt. An emergency fund provides a critical buffer, reducing the financial burden and allowing you to focus on your health and recovery. It can prevent the added stress of navigating complex financial arrangements while dealing with a health crisis. It allows you to concentrate on your well-being, ensuring that your health isn't further compromised by financial worries.

Unexpected car repairs, home repairs, or even unexpected travel expenses can all significantly impact your finances. Without an emergency fund, these expenses could plunge you into debt. With an emergency fund, you can handle these unexpected costs without disrupting your financial stability. You can resolve these issues without resorting to high-interest credit cards or loans, protecting your long-term financial well-being.

In conclusion, building and maintaining an emergency fund is not merely a suggestion; it's a fundamental pillar of long-term financial security. It provides a crucial safety net against unforeseen circumstances, allowing you to navigate unexpected challenges without jeopardizing your financial stability. By implementing the strategies discussed in this section, automating savings, cutting unnecessary spending, and maintaining motivation, you can establish a robust emergency fund that safeguards your financial well-being and provides invaluable peace of mind. Remember, it's about building a secure financial foundation, protecting your future and securing a more stable and confident financial journey. The peace of mind that comes with knowing you have a financial safety net is immeasurable. It's an investment in yourself and your future, enabling you to face life's unexpected events with confidence and resilience.

LongTerm Financial Goal Setting and Review

Now that we've established the critical role of an emergency fund in securing your short-term financial well-being, let's shift our focus to the long game: building long-term financial security. This involves setting ambitious yet achievable long-term financial goals and consistently reviewing and adjusting your strategy to ensure you stay on track. Life is unpredictable, and your financial goals should reflect that adaptability.

Think of your long-term financial planning as a dynamic roadmap, not a rigid itinerary. Your initial route may seem perfectly clear, but unforeseen detours – job changes, unexpected medical expenses, changes in family circumstances – are inevitable. The key is to have a plan, but also the flexibility to re-route as needed, adjusting your strategy without losing sight of your ultimate destination.

Let's start by defining your long-term financial goals. What does financial security look like to you? For some, it might mean owning a home, while for others, it could mean early retirement, funding children's education, or establishing a substantial investment

portfolio. Your goals should be specific, measurable, achievable, relevant, and time-bound – the SMART goal framework. For

example, instead of vaguely aiming to "save for retirement," a SMART goal might be "to accumulate $1 million in retirement savings by age 65."

Once you've defined your goals, break them down into smaller, more manageable steps. This will make the overall objective seem less daunting and provide a sense of accomplishment as you achieve each milestone. For the $1 million retirement goal, you might set intermediate targets like saving $100,000 in the next five years, then $200,000 in the following five, and so on. Each smaller

achievement will fuel your motivation and keep you on track.

Tracking your progress is crucial. Use budgeting tools, spreadsheets, or financial planning software to monitor your savings, investments, and expenses. Regularly review your progress against your goals and make necessary adjustments. This isn't just about numbers; it's about understanding your financial health and making conscious choices. Are you on track to meet your five-year savings goal? If not, where can you adjust your spending or increase your income?

Flexibility is paramount in long-term financial planning. Life throws curveballs. Unexpected events, like job loss or medical emergencies (which your emergency fund helps mitigate), can significantly impact your ability to meet your long-term goals. When such events occur, don't panic. Reassess your goals and adjust your plan accordingly. Perhaps you need to postpone a goal slightly or prioritize different savings targets for a while. The important thing is to maintain your financial discipline and recalibrate your strategy, not abandon your dreams entirely.

Regular review and adjustment are vital. Schedule annual or semi-annual reviews of your long-term financial plan. This is a chance to reflect on your achievements, acknowledge setbacks, and adjust your strategy based on your current circumstances and changing market conditions. Use these reviews as opportunities to learn, adapt, and refine your approach. Perhaps your investment strategy needs tweaking, your savings rate requires a boost, or you need to explore new income streams.

Consider utilizing different financial tools to aid in your long-term planning. Budgeting apps can provide detailed insights into your spending habits, highlighting areas where you can save more effectively. Investment platforms offer diverse options for investing your savings, allowing you to tailor your portfolio to your risk tolerance and long-term goals. Financial planning software can help you model different scenarios and forecast your future financial position, allowing you to proactively address potential challenges.

Let's look at some practical examples. Suppose your long-term goal is to buy a house in five years. You'll need to track your savings progress toward a down payment, monitor changes in interest rates, and research the housing market in your desired location. If interest rates rise unexpectedly, you may need to adjust your savings rate or consider a smaller house. Similarly, if your income fluctuates, you might need to extend your timeframe or explore alternative financing options.

Another example: If your goal is early retirement, you'll need to diligently track your investment returns, adjust your portfolio as needed, and carefully plan for your retirement expenses. Market volatility can impact your investment returns, and unexpected health issues might increase your retirement costs. Regular reviews of your retirement plan allow you to adapt to these challenges, ensuring your plan remains realistic and achievable.

Remember, your financial journey is not a sprint; it's a marathon. There will be obstacles, unexpected expenses, and periods where progress feels slow. The key is consistency, discipline, and the willingness to adjust your strategy as needed. Regular review of your long-term goals allows you to stay focused, motivated, and on track to achieving your financial aspirations.

Don't be afraid to seek professional guidance. A financial advisor can provide personalized advice, create a comprehensive financial plan, and help you navigate complex financial decisions. They can offer objective insights and help you stay accountable, which can be crucial for long-term success. Remember, it's an investment in your future, not an expense.

In addition to professional advice, consider building a support network. Share your goals with trusted friends or family members who can offer encouragement and accountability. Discussing your financial plans with others can help you stay motivated and focused, especially during challenging times. Consider joining online communities or forums where you can connect with like-minded individuals, share experiences, and learn from each other. Financial success is often a shared journey, not a solo endeavor.

Finally, remember that your financial goals are not static. As you progress through life, your circumstances will inevitably change, and your goals should adapt accordingly. Marriage, children, career changes, and unexpected life events can all influence your financial priorities. Regularly reviewing and adjusting your long-term financial plan is not just a good practice; it is essential to ensure that your goals remain aligned with your current circumstances and aspirations. Embrace the journey, celebrate your progress, and remember that your financial security is a continuous process of planning, adaptation, and commitment. This iterative approach, constantly reviewing and adjusting, allows you to maintain

momentum and achieve lasting financial success. The flexibility to adapt and the discipline to consistently review will ultimately be your most valuable assets. Your financial future is a work in progress, not a destination.

Tracking Spending and Identifying Savings Opportunities

Now that we've laid the groundwork for long-term financial

planning, it's time to delve into the nitty-gritty: managing your day-to-day spending. Understanding where your money goes is the first crucial step towards building a strong financial foundation. Many people underestimate the power of small, consistent savings; these seemingly insignificant amounts accumulate significantly over time. Think of it like compound interest, but in reverse: small, consistent overspending compounds into a substantial loss over the long term.

Tracking your spending isn't about deprivation; it's about mindful spending. It's about making conscious choices about how you allocate your resources, ensuring that every dollar spent aligns with your values and long-term financial goals. It's about understanding your spending patterns and identifying areas where you can make adjustments without sacrificing your quality of life.

The most effective way to track your spending is to develop a consistent method. This could involve using budgeting apps,

maintaining a spreadsheet, or even using a simple notebook. The best method is the one you'll actually stick with. Consistency is key.

Choose a method that suits your personality and tech-savviness.

Budgeting apps have become increasingly sophisticated and user-friendly. Many offer features beyond basic expense tracking,

including automated categorization, visual representations of your spending, and even personalized financial advice. Some popular options include Mint, YNAB (You Need A Budget), Personal Capital, and EveryDollar. These apps typically link directly to your bank accounts and credit cards, automatically importing transaction data.

This eliminates the manual entry of each purchase, making the process far more efficient.

If you prefer a more hands-on approach, a simple spreadsheet can be equally effective. You can create columns for date, description, category, and amount. This allows for a high degree of customization; you can tailor the categories to reflect your unique spending patterns. For instance, you might have categories like

"Groceries," "Dining Out," "Transportation," "Entertainment," and "Unexpected Expenses." The advantage of a spreadsheet is its flexibility; you can easily add or modify categories as needed.

For those who prefer a low-tech approach, a simple notebook can work surprisingly well. The act of physically writing down each transaction can increase mindfulness, making you more aware of your spending habits. The disadvantage here is the lack of

automated data entry and the potential for errors. However, this can be overcome with careful organization and regular review.

Regardless of the method you choose, the key is to be thorough. Track every expense, no matter how small. That $3 latte adds up over time, just as much as the larger expenses. The goal is to develop a complete picture of your spending habits. Only then can you begin to identify areas where you can make changes.

Once you've gathered your spending data for a month or two, analyze it carefully. Look for patterns and trends. Are there specific categories where you're consistently overspending? Are there recurring expenses that could be reduced or eliminated? Many people find that identifying areas for improvement can be

surprisingly insightful.

Let's look at some common areas where people find opportunities to save:

Dining Out: Eating out frequently can significantly impact your budget. Consider cooking at home more often, packing lunches, and opting for less expensive dining options when you do eat out. Even small changes like cutting back from three restaurant meals a week to one can make a considerable difference over time.

Subscriptions: Many people subscribe to various services they barely use. Review your subscriptions regularly—streaming

services, gym memberships, software, etc.—and cancel any that are unnecessary or underutilized. You'll be surprised how many recurring charges you might have forgotten about. The cumulative cost of these subscriptions can be staggering over a year.

Transportation: If you have a car, explore ways to reduce your transportation costs. Carpooling, biking, or using public

transportation can save money on gas and vehicle maintenance. If your commute is long, consider relocating closer to your workplace.

Shopping Habits: Impulse purchases and online shopping sprees can quickly deplete your savings. Implement strategies to curb these habits, such as creating shopping lists, avoiding shopping when feeling stressed or emotional, and unfollowing brands or influencers that trigger unwanted spending.

Entertainment: Analyze your entertainment spending. Are you spending too much on movies, concerts, or other forms of

entertainment? Explore less expensive alternatives, such as free community events, outdoor activities, or spending time with friends at home.

Utilities: Analyze your utility bills (electricity, water, gas, internet) and identify ways to reduce consumption. Simple steps like turning off lights when leaving a room, unplugging electronics, and taking shorter showers can significantly lower your monthly bills over time.

Once you've identified areas where you can cut back, create a plan to implement those changes. Start small, focusing on one or two areas at a time. Don't try to overhaul your entire spending habits overnight; this can lead to frustration and failure. Celebrate your successes, no matter how small, to stay motivated.

Tracking your spending and identifying savings opportunities is an ongoing process, not a one-time event. Regularly review your spending habits, adjust your budget as needed, and celebrate your progress. Remember, consistency is key. The small changes you make today will accumulate into significant savings over time, bringing you closer to achieving your long-term financial goals.

Let's consider some real-world examples. Imagine Sarah, a

millennial struggling to save for a down payment on a condo. She used a budgeting app and discovered that she was spending $300 a month on dining out. By reducing this to $100 a month through meal prepping and occasional less expensive outings, she saved $200 monthly, or $2400 annually. This significantly accelerated her savings plan.

Then there's Mark, who used a spreadsheet to track his expenses and realized he was paying for several unused streaming services. Canceling these subscriptions freed up an additional $50 per month.

He then used this saved money to contribute to his investment accounts, further enhancing his long-term financial security. This is about intentional spending, not deprivation.

The key takeaway is this: tracking your spending isn't about restricting yourself; it's about making informed choices. By

understanding your spending patterns, you can identify areas for improvement, freeing up resources to pursue your financial goals.

It's about empowering yourself with knowledge and developing mindful spending habits that will serve you well in the long run. This conscientious approach, combined with consistent tracking and review, will transform your relationship with money, setting you on a path to lasting financial well-being. The journey requires

commitment and effort, but the reward—financial freedom—is well worth the investment. And remember, every small step forward contributes to your overall financial success. Celebrate your

victories along the way!

Cultivating a Savings Mindset

Now that you've mastered the art of tracking your spending and identifying areas for improvement, let's shift our focus to the

equally crucial aspect of cultivating a positive savings mindset. This isn't just about restricting spending; it's about actively cultivating a relationship with your money that prioritizes your future self. Many people struggle with saving not because they lack the income, but because they lack the mental framework to make it a priority. This section will equip you with the tools and strategies to overcome these mental barriers and develop a powerful savings habit.

One of the biggest hurdles to saving is the "out of sight, out of mind" mentality. If you don't see your savings accumulating, it can be easy to lose motivation. To combat this, visualize your financial goals. What are you saving for? A down payment on a house? A dream vacation? Early retirement? Create a vision board, a digital collage, or even just write it down. Make these goals tangible and keep them in front of you as a constant reminder of your "why." This visualization will fuel your motivation and commitment to saving.

Another powerful strategy is to automate your savings. Set up automatic transfers from your checking account to your savings account, ideally on payday. This ensures that a portion of your income is automatically set aside before you even have a chance to spend it. Even small, consistent amounts add up over time. Many banks and online financial institutions offer this feature, making it incredibly easy to implement. Consider setting up multiple

automated transfers, one for your emergency fund, one for short-term goals, and another for long-term investments.

Setting realistic savings goals is crucial to avoid burnout and maintain motivation. Don't try to save everything at once. Start small and gradually increase your savings rate as your income increases and your expenses decrease. Remember, progress, not perfection, is the key. Celebrate small victories along the way to stay motivated. Instead of aiming for a huge lump sum, break your savings goals into smaller, more manageable milestones. This will make the journey less daunting and provide regular opportunities to celebrate your achievements.

Overcoming the psychological barriers to saving often requires addressing ingrained spending habits and emotional attachments to money. For many, shopping provides an emotional outlet, a means of self-soothing or stress relief. Understanding your relationship with money is crucial to making lasting behavioral changes. If you find yourself frequently turning to shopping as a coping mechanism, consider exploring healthier alternatives, like exercise, meditation, or spending time with loved ones. This conscious self-awareness will assist you in identifying your triggers and developing healthy responses.

Furthermore, consider the psychological benefits of saving. Having a financial cushion reduces stress and anxiety. Knowing that you have money set aside for emergencies provides a sense of security and control over your life. This psychological benefit is often overlooked, but it's a powerful motivator. Consider the peace of mind that comes with knowing you can handle unexpected expenses without falling into debt. This sense of security is invaluable.

Let's address some common objections to saving. Many people say they "can't" save because they don't have enough money. This is often a misconception. Saving is not about having a large surplus; it's about making conscious choices about how you spend your money. Even small, consistent savings, coupled with mindful spending habits, can add up significantly over time. The power of compound interest will work its magic, turning small amounts into substantial sums over the long term.

Another frequent objection is that saving feels like deprivation. This is a misconception as well. Saving is not about sacrificing your happiness; it's about prioritizing your long-term well-being. By making conscious choices about how you spend your money, you can still enjoy your life while simultaneously building a secure financial future. It's a matter of shifting your mindset from

immediate gratification to long-term fulfillment.

Let’s consider the concept of “paying yourself first.” This involves automatically allocating a portion of your income to savings before paying any other bills or expenses. This establishes savings as a non-negotiable priority. This simple mental shift can drastically impact your savings rate. Treat your savings as a non-negotiable expense, just like rent or utilities. This prioritization ensures your future self is taken care of.

Practical tips for saving money on everyday expenses can further enhance your savings efforts. Consider bringing your lunch to work instead of eating out every day. This seemingly small change can accumulate substantial savings over a month or year. Utilize coupons and discount codes when shopping online. Explore less expensive entertainment options, such as free community events or outdoor activities. These changes will contribute meaningfully to your financial well-being.

Saving money on utilities can also significantly boost your savings. Simple adjustments, like turning off lights when leaving a room or unplugging electronics, can make a difference. Similarly, conserving water and reducing your energy consumption will lead to lower bills. These seemingly small changes, when consistently implemented, can result in remarkable savings over time.

Finally, remember that saving is a marathon, not a sprint. Don't get discouraged by setbacks. There will be months when you can save more, and months when you can save less. The key is consistency. Even if you can only save a small amount each month, it is still a significant step toward building a secure financial future. Celebrate small victories and maintain a long-term perspective.

The journey toward cultivating a positive savings mindset is a personal one. It's about understanding your relationship with money, identifying your spending triggers, and developing strategies to overcome those hurdles. By combining mindful spending with automated savings, you can create a powerful system that works for you, ensuring you steadily move closer to achieving your financial goals. Remember, every small step you take today will contribute to the accumulation of wealth and the realization of your long-term dreams. The financial freedom that awaits is well worth the effort. Believe in your ability to achieve it, and celebrate every milestone along the way. You've got this!

Smart Shopping Strategies

Now that we've established a strong foundation for saving, let's dive into the practical strategies for smart shopping. Smart shopping isn't about deprivation; it's about making conscious choices that align with your financial goals. It's about maximizing value and minimizing waste, ensuring you get the most for your money without sacrificing your lifestyle.

One of the most effective strategies is mastering the art of comparison shopping. Before making any significant purchase, take the time to compare prices from different retailers. This might involve checking multiple online stores, visiting brick-and-mortar locations, or utilizing price comparison websites. The few minutes you spend comparing prices can save you substantial sums in the long run. Consider the example of a new laptop: a quick online search might reveal a price difference of hundreds of dollars between different retailers, offering the same specifications. This illustrates the potential savings of diligent price comparison. Don't limit your comparison to just the initial price; consider factors like shipping costs, warranty coverage, and return policies. A slightly higher upfront cost might be offset by a superior warranty or easier return process. Factor in these variables for a truly comprehensive comparison.

Beyond comparing prices, actively seek out deals and discounts. This involves utilizing coupons, both physical and digital. Many grocery stores and retail chains offer loyalty programs that provide discounts and exclusive offers to members. Sign up for these programs, as they often translate into significant savings over time. Check your email inbox regularly for promotional offers and discount codes. Many online retailers provide exclusive discounts to email subscribers.

Furthermore, consider timing your purchases strategically. Many retailers offer significant discounts during holiday sales, end-of-season clearances, and flash sales. Plan your purchases around these periods to maximize your savings. Researching sales calendars for specific items you need can significantly reduce your spending.

Don't impulsively buy something just because it is on sale. If you don't need the item, the discount is irrelevant.

Another crucial aspect of smart shopping is resisting impulse buys.

Impulse purchases are often the biggest culprits in overspending. Before making a purchase, pause and ask yourself if you truly need the item. Often, the initial desire fades quickly, leaving you with an unnecessary expense. A useful technique is to wait 24 hours before making any non-essential purchase. This delay often allows the initial urge to subside, giving you a clearer perspective on the purchase's necessity. If you still want the item after 24 hours, you can revisit the decision with a cooler head.

Develop a shopping list and stick to it. This simple technique is remarkably effective in preventing impulse buys and reducing spending. Before heading to the grocery store or any retail location, create a detailed list of items you need. This disciplined approach will keep you focused on essential purchases and avoid impulse buys. Utilize the shopping list as a guide, and only deviate from it with conscious deliberation.

Consider the long-term costs of a purchase. Often, we focus on the initial price of an item, overlooking the ongoing costs. For instance, purchasing a cheaper car might seem economical upfront, but higher maintenance and fuel costs could outweigh the initial

savings. Therefore, factor in the total cost of ownership, including maintenance, repairs, and operating expenses, before committing to a significant purchase. This holistic perspective will prevent

impulsive spending on short-sighted purchases.

Grocery shopping deserves special attention. Planning your meals ahead of time is crucial in reducing grocery waste and costs. A well-planned meal plan prevents buying excess food that might spoil before you have a chance to consume it. Consider purchasing generic brands, which are often significantly cheaper than name brands, without compromising quality. Take advantage of store coupons and loyalty programs to further reduce your grocery bill.

Consider bulk buying for frequently used items, such as non-perishable staples, provided you have sufficient storage space.

Saving money on clothing requires a strategic approach. Consider buying versatile clothing items that can be mixed and matched. This will reduce the need to purchase a large number of individual pieces. Look for high-quality clothing items that will last longer, reducing the need for frequent replacements. Shop during sales and clearances, but only for items you truly need. Avoid being swayed by fleeting trends.

Entertainment costs can also add up significantly. Explore less expensive entertainment options such as free community events, outdoor activities, or library resources. Take advantage of free trials for streaming services before committing to a paid subscription.

Avoid paying full price for movie tickets by utilizing discount programs or attending matinee showings. Utilize free or low-cost apps and websites for entertainment. These options not only save money but also promote creative ways to spend your time.

Let's look at some real-life examples. Sarah, a young professional, implemented smart shopping strategies and reduced her monthly spending by 20% within three months. She started by creating a detailed budget, tracking her expenses meticulously. Then she transitioned to comparison shopping before making significant purchases. She utilized coupons and loyalty programs, planned her meals to reduce grocery waste, and prioritized purchasing quality over quantity when buying clothing. She found alternatives to expensive entertainment such as attending free community events and utilizing her local library. Her disciplined approach and

conscious choices led to substantial savings.

John, another millennial, struggled with impulse buying. He

adopted the 24-hour rule and made a conscious effort to slow down his shopping habits. He also started creating detailed shopping lists. This combination of strategies dramatically reduced his impulsive spending. Instead of instantly purchasing items he craved, he deliberated on their actual necessity. This pause allowed him to re-evaluate his needs, resulting in greater control over his spending.

Smart shopping isn't about sacrificing your lifestyle; it's about making informed choices that align with your financial priorities. By implementing the strategies discussed—comparison shopping, utilizing coupons, resisting impulse purchases, and developing mindful shopping habits—you can significantly reduce your

expenses and free up more money to save and invest. Remember, the journey toward financial freedom is a marathon, not a sprint. Celebrate small victories along the way, and stay committed to your financial goals. Every conscious decision you make, every dollar you save, moves you closer to achieving long-term financial security and fulfilling your dreams.

Negotiating Better Deals and Avoiding Overspending

Building upon the foundation of smart shopping strategies, let's now delve into the powerful skill of negotiation and the art of avoiding those sneaky overspending traps. Negotiating isn't about being aggressive or confrontational; it's about respectfully advocating for yourself and securing the best possible value for your money. It's a skill that can be learned and honed, significantly impacting your overall financial well-being.

First, understand that negotiation is a two-way street. It's not about winning or losing; it's about finding a mutually beneficial

agreement. Before approaching a negotiation, research the market value of the product or service you're interested in. Knowing the going rate empowers you to confidently propose a fair price.

Websites and apps dedicated to price comparison, consumer reviews, and product specifications can be invaluable resources in this research phase. Don't hesitate to spend time comparing

offerings, as this research can save you hundreds, even thousands, of dollars.

For larger purchases, such as cars, furniture, or electronics, don't be afraid to haggle. Many retailers have built-in wiggle room in their pricing, anticipating negotiation. Start by politely inquiring about any potential discounts or special offers. Mentioning competing offers from other retailers can be a powerful negotiating tactic, demonstrating your awareness of market prices. Be prepared to walk away if the seller isn't willing to compromise, as this can often be the most effective bargaining chip. Remember, patience is key. A good deal is worth the wait.

When negotiating, maintain a respectful and professional demeanor. Avoid aggressive tactics, as these can damage the relationship and hinder your chances of reaching a favorable agreement. Instead, focus on building rapport with the seller. A friendly and collaborative approach is far more likely to yield positive results than a confrontational one. Clearly articulate your needs and expectations, while remaining flexible and open to compromise.

Let's consider a practical example. Imagine you're purchasing a new washing machine. After researching online, you discover the

average price is around $600. You visit a local appliance store and find a model you like, priced at $700. Instead of accepting the listed price, you politely ask the salesperson if any discounts are available.

You mention seeing a similar model for $650 at a competitor's store. The salesperson, wanting to secure the sale, might offer a price reduction of $25-$50, or throw in an extended warranty or free delivery. This seemingly small discount translates to significant savings over the lifespan of the appliance.

Beyond tangible goods, the principles of negotiation apply equally to services. Whether it's negotiating a lower monthly rent, securing a better interest rate on a loan, or haggling with a contractor, the same core principles remain relevant. Thorough research is

essential. Understanding the market rate for the service you require allows you to make informed and confident proposals. Be clear about your expectations and budget, and be prepared to justify your offers. Demonstrate your willingness to compromise, while also standing your ground on key issues.

Beyond negotiation, understanding and avoiding overspending pitfalls is paramount. Many of these traps stem from impulsive decisions and a lack of awareness of our spending habits. One of the most potent weapons against overspending is the art of mindful spending. This involves consciously analyzing each purchase before committing. Ask yourself, “Do I really need this?” or “Can I afford this without impacting my financial goals?” These simple questions can prevent many impulse purchases.

Another sneaky overspending trap is the allure of "deals" that are not actual deals. A "$50 off" sticker can be misleading if the original price was significantly inflated. Always verify the actual savings before making a purchase. Compare prices across different retailers, websites, and even used markets, to ensure you are indeed getting a good deal.

Don't be swayed by aggressive sales tactics or high-pressure salespersons. Take your time, consider the total cost of ownership (including warranties, maintenance, and potential long-term expenses) and make an informed decision.

Credit card debt is another major contributor to overspending.

High-interest rates can quickly spiral out of control, significantly hindering your progress toward financial freedom. Strive to pay off credit card balances in full each month, avoiding interest charges. If you're carrying a balance, prioritize paying off the debt as quickly as possible, focusing on high-interest debt first. Budgeting and mindful spending will drastically reduce the chance of running into credit card debt, allowing you to reap the benefits of interest-free spending.

Subscription services, while convenient, are a sneaky way to overspend. Review your subscriptions regularly, canceling any you rarely use or no longer need. This seemingly minor adjustment can result in significant long-term savings. Consider utilizing free or lower-cost alternatives for entertainment, news, and

communication.

Emotional spending is a common overspending pitfall. When feeling stressed, sad, or bored, we often turn to shopping as a temporary fix. Recognizing this emotional trigger and developing healthy coping mechanisms, such as exercise, meditation, or spending time with loved ones, is crucial in managing emotional spending. Create a strategy for addressing stress in a way that does not involve financial indulgence.

Regularly review your bank statements and credit card statements, monitoring your spending patterns. Identify areas where you are overspending and strategize ways to curb those expenditures. Financial tracking apps and budgeting software can be extremely helpful in this process, providing insights into your spending habits and helping you set realistic financial goals. Utilize the data these apps give you to spot trends and address unnecessary expenses.

Cultivating a savings-oriented mindset is a crucial component of both negotiation and preventing overspending. This mindset shifts your focus from immediate gratification to long-term financial security. By viewing savings as an investment in your future, you are more likely to prioritize it over immediate wants. Remember, every dollar you save is a step closer to your financial goals.

Finally, remember that achieving financial success is a journey, not a destination. There will be setbacks and occasional overspending, but don't let these derail you. Learn from your mistakes, adapt your strategies, and continue to strive towards your financial objectives.

Celebrate small victories along the way, acknowledging and

reinforcing positive financial habits. Consistent effort and conscious decision-making will ultimately lead to long-term financial well-being.

Debt Management and Avoidance

Building on the principles of mindful spending and negotiation, let's now turn our attention to a critical aspect of personal finance: debt management and avoidance. While negotiation helps you secure better deals and prevent overspending, proactive debt management ensures you stay in control of your finances and avoid the crippling weight of debt. Many young adults find themselves burdened by student loans, credit card debt, or medical bills, making the journey to financial freedom a daunting climb. But with a strategic

approach, you can navigate these challenges and build a solid financial foundation.

The first step towards effective debt management is a

comprehensive understanding of your current financial situation. This involves meticulously tracking all your income and expenses, identifying your sources of debt, and determining the interest rates associated with each. A simple spreadsheet or a budgeting app can be incredibly helpful in this process. Once you have a clear picture of your financial landscape, you can start developing a plan to tackle your debt.

Responsible credit card usage is paramount. Credit cards can be valuable financial tools, offering convenience and rewards

programs. However, they can also be a significant source of debt if not managed carefully. Always strive to pay your credit card

balance in full each month. This avoids accruing interest charges, which can quickly escalate your debt. If you're unable to pay the full balance, make at least the minimum payment and prioritize paying down the highest-interest debt first. This strategy, known as the avalanche method, minimizes the total amount of interest you pay over time. Alternatively, the snowball method focuses on paying off the smallest debt first for a quick sense of

accomplishment, which can boost morale during the debt

repayment process.

Understanding your credit score is crucial. Your credit score is a three-digit number that lenders use to assess your creditworthiness. A higher credit score typically translates to better interest rates and more favorable lending terms. Factors influencing your credit score include payment history (the most significant factor), amounts owed, length of credit history, new credit, and credit mix. Regularly monitoring your credit report, available for free through

AnnualCreditReport.com, allows you to identify and address any errors or inaccuracies that could negatively impact your score.

Dispute any errors you find promptly with the credit bureaus.

Maintaining a healthy credit score is essential for securing loans, renting an apartment, or even getting a job in certain industries. It significantly reduces the stress and higher costs associated with borrowing money.

Beyond credit cards, other types of debt require careful

management. Student loans, often a significant financial burden for young adults, require a strategic repayment plan. Explore different repayment options, such as income-driven repayment plans, which adjust your monthly payments based on your income. Consolidate your student loans to simplify payments and potentially lower your interest rate. For medical bills, negotiate payment plans with

healthcare providers or explore options for financial assistance programs. Don't hesitate to contact the provider's billing department to discuss payment options. They may be willing to work with you to create a manageable payment plan or even reduce the cost of your bill. Transparency and proactive communication are key to achieving a positive outcome. Many medical providers have

financial assistance programs to support patients.

Avoid accumulating further debt by creating a realistic budget and sticking to it. A well-defined budget helps you track your income and expenses, identifying areas where you can cut back and save money. Allocate funds for debt repayment as a priority, ensuring you consistently make your payments on time and in full. Regularly review your budget and make adjustments as needed to reflect any changes in your income or expenses. A detailed monthly budget is essential for controlling your financial situation. Track your

spending in detail to see where your money is going. Categorizing your expenses – necessities, wants, and debt payments – can reveal areas for improvement.

Beyond budgeting, consider strategies to increase your income.

Explore opportunities for freelance work, side hustles, or a part-time job to supplement your income and accelerate your debt repayment efforts. Every extra dollar earned can be directed toward paying down debt, shortening the time it takes to become debt-free. Investing your money wisely can help increase your wealth, offering a long-term strategy to alleviate financial pressures.

Debt consolidation can be a valuable tool for managing multiple debts. Consolidating your debts into a single loan can simplify your payments and potentially reduce your interest rate, making it easier to manage your finances and accelerate repayment. Shop around for the best consolidation loan terms and compare interest rates and fees before making a decision. Be aware of the terms and conditions, making sure the consolidation loan doesn't come with hidden fees or unfavorable terms.

In addition to responsible borrowing and repayment, building an emergency fund is a critical component of effective debt management. An emergency fund provides a safety net for unexpected expenses, such as medical bills or car repairs, preventing you from accumulating more debt when facing unforeseen circumstances. Aim to save at least three to six months'worth of living expenses in an easily accessible savings account. This will prevent you from resorting to credit cards or other loans when facing financial emergencies.

Finally, remember that achieving financial freedom is a marathon, not a sprint. There will be setbacks and challenges along the way, but don't let them discourage you. Stay committed to your debt repayment plan, celebrate your progress, and don't hesitate to seek professional financial advice if needed. Financial advisors can provide personalized guidance and support to help you create a debt management plan that aligns with your individual circumstances and financial goals. They can help you navigate complex financial situations and make informed decisions about your debt. Remember, you're not alone in this journey. Numerous resources and support systems are available to help you overcome debt and achieve financial well-being. Taking proactive steps, and consistently working towards your financial goals, will eventually lead you to a more secure and prosperous future.

Understanding Credit Scores and Reports

Understanding your credit score is fundamental to building a strong financial foundation. It's a three-digit number that acts as a shorthand summary of your creditworthiness, influencing everything from the interest rates you qualify for on loans to your ability to rent an apartment. Lenders, landlords, and even some employers use this score to assess your risk – essentially, how likely you are to repay borrowed money. A higher score generally translates to better financial opportunities, while a low score can significantly limit your options and potentially cost you thousands of dollars in higher interest rates over time.

Think of your credit score like your financial reputation. It's a reflection of your past borrowing and repayment behavior. Each time you apply for credit, make a payment, or even have a late payment reported, that information is recorded and contributes to your overall credit score. This score is calculated by the three major credit bureaus: Equifax, Experian, and TransUnion. While each bureau may have slightly different scoring models, they all consider similar factors. Understanding these factors is crucial for improving and maintaining a healthy credit score.

The most significant factor affecting your credit score is your payment history. This accounts for approximately 35% of your score. Consistent, on-time payments demonstrate your reliability as a borrower. Even one late payment can negatively impact your score, and multiple late payments can severely damage it. Make timely payments a priority, setting up automatic payments or reminders if necessary. Avoid bouncing checks or missing payments altogether – these actions can significantly hurt your credit score and make it harder to secure loans or credit in the future.

The amounts you owe, representing approximately 30% of your credit score, is another crucial factor. This refers to your credit utilization ratio – the percentage of your available credit that you're currently using. Keeping your credit utilization low, ideally below 30%, signals responsible credit management. High credit utilization suggests you might be overextending yourself financially, increasing your risk profile for lenders. For example, if you have a credit card with a $1,000 limit, try to keep your balance below $300. Paying down your balances regularly and strategically managing your credit limits will keep this aspect of your score healthy.

The length of your credit history accounts for 15% of your credit score. A longer history of responsible credit use demonstrates consistent financial stability and trustworthiness. This is why it's important to start building credit early, even with a small credit card with a low credit limit. Avoid closing old accounts unless absolutely necessary, as this can shorten your credit history and potentially lower your score. Longer accounts with a consistent history of on-time payments are advantageous. As your credit history grows, your score tends to improve, reflecting your sustained responsible financial behavior over time.

New credit applications comprise 10% of your credit score. Each time you apply for a new credit card or loan, an inquiry is placed on your credit report. Too many inquiries in a short period can suggest you're facing financial hardship or are struggling to manage your finances. While a single inquiry won't drastically affect your score, multiple inquiries within a short timeframe can hurt your credit score. This is because each inquiry represents a potential risk for lenders. Try to limit your applications for new credit to those absolutely needed.

Finally, your credit mix contributes 10% to your credit score. This refers to the variety of credit accounts you hold – credit cards, installment loans (like auto loans or student loans), and mortgages. Having a mix of different credit accounts demonstrates your ability to manage various types of credit responsibly. However, it's more important to manage existing accounts responsibly than to actively seek out diverse credit types to boost your score. Focus on

responsible use and timely payments rather than striving for a specific mix of credit accounts.

Understanding your credit report is equally important as

understanding your credit score. Your credit report is a detailed record of your credit history, providing a comprehensive view of your borrowing and repayment behavior. You can obtain your free credit reports annually from AnnualCreditReport.com, the only authorized website for free reports under the Fair Credit Reporting Act. Review your reports carefully for any inaccuracies or errors. Even seemingly minor errors can negatively impact your score, so it's crucial to promptly dispute any discrepancies you find with the respective credit bureaus.

Interpreting your credit report requires understanding the information presented. Familiarize yourself with the different sections, including your personal information, accounts (credit cards, loans, etc.), public records (bankruptcies, judgments), and inquiries (credit applications). Each entry should reflect accurately on your credit history. Pay particular attention to the status of your accounts—whether they're open or closed, current or delinquent, and any associated payment histories. Scrutinize the details of each account to ensure accuracy.

Beyond understanding your credit score and report, actively working to improve them is crucial. Paying bills on time is the most straightforward method to enhance your credit score. This consistently demonstrates reliability and responsible credit management. Regularly monitoring your credit utilization ratio is also critical. Aim to keep your balances significantly below your credit limits—below 30% is generally recommended. This signals sound financial management and reduces the perception of risk to lenders.

Consider consolidating high-interest debt. High-interest debt can make it harder to manage your finances and can negatively impact your credit score. Consolidating multiple debts into a single loan with a lower interest rate can simplify payments and improve your credit utilization ratio. This is especially beneficial if you have several debts with high interest rates. Lowering your interest payments frees up funds that can be used to pay down your debt faster, while simultaneously improving your score.

Avoid applying for too much new credit within a short period. Each new credit application results in an inquiry on your credit report, potentially reducing your score if you have numerous inquiries over time. Limit applications to those essential to your needs and financial goals. This helps to maintain a healthy credit profile.

Dispute any errors found on your credit reports. It's important to regularly review your credit reports for errors. If you find any inaccuracies, dispute them promptly with the respective credit bureaus. Inaccuracies can negatively impact your score, potentially limiting financial opportunities.

Maintaining a healthy credit score is an ongoing process, requiring consistent effort and attention. It affects your access to credit, the interest rates you'll receive, and even your ability to rent an

apartment or secure certain jobs. By understanding the factors that contribute to your credit score, monitoring your reports, and actively working to improve your credit health, you can build a strong financial foundation and unlock better financial

opportunities in the future. Remember, a good credit score is a valuable asset, paving the way for a more secure and prosperous financial future. The effort invested now will reap significant rewards in the years to come.

Building a Positive Credit History

Building a positive credit history is more than just a number; it's the cornerstone of your financial future. It's the silent partner that negotiates better interest rates on loans, unlocks rental

opportunities, and even influences your chances in certain job applications. Think of it as your financial reputation – a testament to your responsible borrowing and repayment habits. While the previous section delved into understanding your credit score and report, this section focuses on the practical steps you can take to actively cultivate and nurture a positive credit history.

The most fundamental aspect of building a positive credit history is consistent, on-time bill payments. This is the single most influential factor, contributing significantly to your creditworthiness. Imagine this: you've secured a loan for a new car. Every month, you

meticulously ensure the payment is made on or before the due date. This consistent reliability demonstrates to lenders your commitment to fulfilling financial obligations. Conversely, even a single late payment can cast a shadow on your otherwise pristine credit

record. This single lapse can trigger a decrease in your credit score, potentially affecting your ability to secure favorable terms on future loans or credit cards. Late payments communicate to lenders a higher risk profile, leading them to charge higher interest rates to compensate for perceived uncertainty. Establish a system to track your due dates; set calendar reminders, use automatic payments, or consider budgeting apps that send payment alerts.

Beyond timely payments, managing your credit card balances effectively is paramount. Avoid maxing out your credit cards.

Lenders closely scrutinize your credit utilization ratio – the

percentage of your available credit you're currently using. Keeping this ratio low, ideally under 30%, projects financial responsibility. A high utilization ratio, on the other hand, signals potential financial strain. For example, if you have a credit card with a $5,000 limit, aiming to keep your balance below $1,500 demonstrates

responsible spending habits. Regularly paying down your credit card balances is critical. Consider setting up automatic payments to ensure consistent progress towards a lower balance. Strategic management of your credit limits can also be advantageous. Avoid requesting unnecessary credit limit increases unless you have a specific need and the capacity to manage the increased available credit. If possible, consider gradually paying off your balances to lower your credit utilization even further.

Understanding the different types of credit is another important aspect of building a robust credit history. While credit cards are a common entry point, diversifying your credit mix can also be beneficial. This means having a combination of credit cards,

installment loans (like auto loans or student loans), and potentially even a mortgage in the future. A diverse credit profile shows lenders you can responsibly manage different types of credit

obligations. This diversity isn't about actively seeking out every loan type possible; rather, it's about allowing your credit history to organically develop as your financial needs evolve. For instance, taking out a student loan for your education, followed by an auto loan for a vehicle, and later securing a mortgage for a home, demonstrates a history of responsible borrowing across various financial products.

Let's illustrate the benefits with some real-life examples. Imagine two young professionals, Sarah and John, both applying for a mortgage. Sarah has consistently made on-time payments on her credit cards and student loans for the past five years, maintaining a low credit utilization ratio. Her credit report reflects a long history of responsible credit management. John, on the other hand, has a history of late payments and high credit utilization. While both want the same mortgage, Sarah is much more likely to secure a favorable interest rate due to her positive credit history. This difference in interest rates can translate to thousands of dollars saved over the life of the loan. This scenario highlights the long-term financial implications of establishing a positive credit history early on. This careful management can unlock financial

opportunities that otherwise remain unattainable.

Beyond the major factors discussed, several other nuances

contribute to building a solid credit foundation. These include avoiding unnecessary credit inquiries. Every time you apply for a new credit card or loan, a hard inquiry appears on your credit report. Numerous hard inquiries within a short period can negatively impact your credit score, signaling potential financial instability. Limit your applications to those truly needed. If you're shopping around for the best interest rate on a loan, consider doing so within a short timeframe (usually 14-45 days) as many credit scoring models will treat these as a single inquiry.

Regularly reviewing your credit reports is essential. You are entitled to a free credit report from each of the three major credit bureaus (Equifax, Experian, and TransUnion) annually through AnnualCreditReport.com. Carefully examine these reports for any inaccuracies or errors. Disputes should be promptly filed with the respective bureau if you find any mistakes. Even minor discrepancies can have significant repercussions on your score, potentially affecting your ability to secure credit or loans. A diligent review ensures the accuracy of your credit report, which is foundational to maintaining a positive credit history.

Remember, building a positive credit history is a marathon, not a sprint. It's a continuous process that requires consistent attention and responsible financial habits. This involves consistently making on-time payments, maintaining a low credit utilization ratio, diversifying your credit mix (over time), and monitoring your credit reports for accuracy. By diligently implementing these strategies, you are investing in your financial future, securing better terms on loans, maximizing your borrowing capacity, and cultivating a strong financial foundation. The financial rewards of a positive credit history are substantial, far outweighing the effort involved in building and maintaining it. It's an investment that continues to pay dividends throughout your life. Start today, build your credit responsibly, and enjoy the long-term financial benefits of a stellar credit score. The future you will thank you for it.

Protecting Your Identity and Financial Information

Protecting your financial well-being extends beyond managing credit scores and debt; it necessitates a robust defense against identity theft and fraud. In today's digital age, where our financial lives are increasingly intertwined with online platforms and digital transactions, safeguarding personal information is paramount. This isn't about paranoia; it's about proactive risk management. A single breach can unravel years of financial progress, leading to significant stress, time investment in recovery, and potential long-term

financial repercussions.

The first line of defense is establishing strong and unique

passwords. Avoid easily guessable passwords like birthdays, pet names, or sequential numbers. Instead, opt for complex passwords that incorporate a combination of uppercase and lowercase letters, numbers, and symbols. A password manager can be an invaluable tool, generating strong passwords and securely storing them,

eliminating the need to remember dozens of complex combinations.

However, remember that the security of your password manager depends on a strong master password; treat this master password with the utmost care, and ensure it is different from all other passwords you utilize. Consider using a different, equally strong, password for your email accounts as this is often the first target for hackers attempting to gain access to your other online accounts.

Beyond password strength, two-factor authentication (2FA) is a critical layer of security. 2FA adds an extra step to the login

process, requiring a second form of verification beyond your

password. This could involve a code sent to your phone, a biometric scan, or a security key. Enabling 2FA on all your financial accounts—including banking, investment, and credit card accounts—

significantly reduces the risk of unauthorized access, even if your password is compromised. Don't underestimate the power of this simple but highly effective security measure.

Regularly monitoring your credit reports is not simply beneficial for maintaining a good credit score, but it's also a crucial step in

identity theft detection. As previously mentioned, you're entitled to a free credit report from each of the three major credit bureaus (Equifax, Experian, and TransUnion) annually through

AnnualCreditReport.com. However, consider checking your reports more frequently – perhaps quarterly – to catch any suspicious activity early. Any unfamiliar accounts, loans, or credit inquiries should be immediately investigated and reported. Prompt action is vital to minimizing potential damage. Consider using a credit

monitoring service, which often provide alerts on suspicious activity and other helpful features that can aid in the early detection and resolution of potential identity theft. Note that these services

generally come with a monthly fee, but the cost is far outweighed by the security and peace of mind they provide.

Secure your physical documents as diligently as you secure your digital information. Shred sensitive documents like bank statements, credit card offers, and tax returns before disposing of them. This prevents unauthorized individuals from accessing your personal and financial details. Regularly review your bank and credit card

statements for any unfamiliar transactions. Report any suspicious activity immediately to your bank or credit card company. Many banks offer transaction alerts which can notify you of potential fraudulent activity. Consider taking advantage of these alerts to receive immediate notifications on any unusual activity with your account.

Phishing scams are a common tactic used by identity thieves. These are deceptive emails, text messages, or phone calls that attempt to trick you into revealing your personal information. Be wary of unsolicited communication requesting sensitive information,

particularly login credentials or financial details. Legitimate

institutions will never ask for your password or other sensitive information via email or text message. If you receive a suspicious communication, do not click on any links or reply to the message. Instead, contact the institution directly using the official contact information found on their website or on your account statements.

Be cautious about the information you share online. Avoid posting sensitive information like your social security number, bank account details, or credit card numbers on social media or other public forums. Think before you share – what information is necessary to share, and what could potentially be used to compromise your identity? Similarly, be mindful of public Wi-Fi networks. Avoid accessing sensitive financial information on unsecured Wi-Fi, as your data could be intercepted by malicious actors. Opt for a Virtual Private Network (VPN) if you need to access your accounts while using a public network. The extra layer of encryption significantly increases your online security.

In the event of identity theft, your immediate response is crucial to mitigating the damage. First, file a police report documenting the theft. This report will be essential when you contact credit bureaus and financial institutions. Next, contact the three major credit bureaus (Equifax, Experian, and TransUnion) and place a fraud alert or security freeze on your credit reports. A fraud alert informs creditors of the potential for fraudulent activity, prompting them to take extra precautions before granting credit. A security freeze prevents new accounts from being opened in your name without your explicit authorization. You'll need to temporarily lift the freeze when applying for legitimate credit.

Contact your financial institutions—banks, credit card companies, and investment firms—and report the theft, closing any compromised accounts and requesting new cards and account numbers. This ensures that any fraudulent transactions are stopped and prevents further misuse of your financial information. Review your credit reports regularly for any unauthorized accounts or activity, even after you've taken steps to resolve the situation. Many financial institutions offer identity theft insurance, or it might be an added benefit included in your credit card or bank account. Check your policy documents to determine the protection it offers in case of identity theft.

Beyond these immediate actions, consider obtaining credit monitoring services to continually monitor your credit reports for any further unauthorized activity. This proactive approach helps ensure that any new fraudulent activity is quickly detected and addressed, minimizing the potential financial impact. Furthermore, consult with a credit repair specialist or financial advisor for

guidance on navigating the complexities of identity recovery and to establish appropriate steps to rebuild your credit if necessary.

Remember, recovery from identity theft can take time and effort, but with proactive measures and prompt action, you can minimize the damage and restore your financial standing.

Protecting your identity and financial information isn't a one-time task; it's an ongoing process that requires vigilance and proactive measures. By diligently implementing the strategies outlined above–strong passwords, two-factor authentication, regular monitoring of your credit reports, secure disposal of documents, and awareness of phishing scams – you're investing in your long-term financial security. Remember, prevention is always better than cure, and a proactive approach to protecting your information will safeguard your financial future and provide you with greater peace of mind.

The efforts invested in securing your personal and financial

information are far outweighed by the potential consequences of a security breach. Make the effort, and secure your financial future.

Financial Literacy Resources and Tools

Building a strong financial foundation requires more than just saving and investing; it demands a solid understanding of personal finance. This section acts as your roadmap to acquiring that

knowledge, providing a curated list of resources designed to boost your financial literacy. Whether you prefer online learning,

interactive apps, or the traditional feel of a good book, there are countless options available, many of which are free or low-cost. The key is finding the resources that best fit your learning style and addressing your specific financial needs.

Let's start with online resources. The internet offers a wealth of information, but it's crucial to be discerning and only utilize

reputable sources. Government websites, such as the Consumer Financial Protection Bureau (CFPB) website, provide unbiased and reliable information on various financial topics. The CFPB offers a vast library of articles, guides, and educational materials covering everything from budgeting and saving to credit management and debt relief. Their website is user-friendly and provides clear, concise explanations, even for complex financial concepts. Furthermore, the CFPB's website provides access to helpful tools and calculators that can assist you in making informed financial decisions. For instance, their debt calculator can help you estimate how long it will take to pay off your debts based on your current repayment plan. Similarly, their savings calculator can illustrate how your savings will grow over time, depending on your contribution amount and interest rate. This interactive approach to learning can significantly enhance your understanding and empower you to make sound decisions.

Beyond government websites, many reputable non-profit

organizations provide free financial education resources. The

National Foundation for Credit Counseling (NFCC), for example, offers a range of resources on budgeting, debt management, and credit repair. They also provide access to certified credit counselors who can provide personalized guidance and support. Many local libraries also offer free workshops and seminars on various financial topics, sometimes in collaboration with these non-profit organizations. Checking your local library's events calendar is a great way to discover free, in-person learning opportunities. These workshops offer a hands-on learning environment, providing the chance to ask questions and interact with financial experts and peers. You may also find local credit unions or community banks offering similar free workshops within the community.

Moving onto mobile applications, there's a plethora of budgeting and personal finance apps designed to simplify money management.

Many of these apps offer free versions with basic features, while premium versions unlock more advanced tools and analysis.

Popular options include Mint, Personal Capital, and YNAB (You Need A Budget). Mint provides an overview of your finances by connecting to your bank accounts and credit cards, automatically categorizing your transactions, and offering insights into your spending habits. Personal Capital goes a step further, offering investment tracking and retirement planning tools, in addition to budgeting and money management features. YNAB adopts a more proactive budgeting approach, requiring you to allocate your income before spending, helping you gain better control of your finances. While these apps vary in their features and approaches, they all aim to empower you with better understanding and control of your money. Carefully compare their features, and consider which best suits your financial needs and personal preferences.

Books remain a valuable resource for building financial literacy.

From classic personal finance guides like "The Total Money

Makeover" by Dave Ramsey to newer titles focusing on specific aspects of personal finance such as investing or debt management, you can find countless books to suit your individual interests and goals. Consider reading books with different perspectives, as this will enrich your understanding and help you refine your approach to personal finance. A well-written book can provide a

comprehensive understanding of a specific financial topic, offering insights and strategies that can be immediately applied to your situation. Furthermore, books can be beneficial for slower and more deliberate learners, offering an alternative to the quick-paced nature of online learning or app-based resources. Libraries again offer a fantastic, free resource for exploring different books,

allowing you to sample several before purchasing any.

Beyond individual resources, consider attending financial literacy workshops or seminars. Many community organizations, colleges, and universities offer free or low-cost workshops on various financial topics. These events often provide a valuable opportunity to learn from financial experts and network with other individuals striving to improve their financial well-being. These workshops can provide a more interactive learning experience and offer a platform to ask questions and clarify any uncertainties. Attending these events can provide you with more holistic approach to learning, encompassing different aspects of personal finance, helping you to identify and address any potential weaknesses in your approach. Check your local community center, university, or college websites for upcoming events.

Remember, financial literacy is an ongoing journey, not a destination. Continuously seeking new knowledge and refining your understanding of personal finance will pay dividends in the long run. Don't be afraid to explore different resources and experiment with different learning approaches. Find what works best for you, and develop a consistent learning habit that aligns with your lifestyle and interests. This continuous learning will not only help you manage your current financial situation but will also equip you with the knowledge and confidence to navigate future financial challenges and opportunities. By actively seeking out and engaging with these resources, you're making a significant investment in your financial future – an investment that will pay off in increased financial security, stability, and peace of mind.

Don't overlook the power of mentorship. If possible, seek out a mentor who has successfully navigated the complexities of personal finance. Their experience and guidance can provide invaluable insights and support, helping you avoid common pitfalls and accelerate your progress. This mentoring relationship can be particularly beneficial when facing complex financial decisions, offering personalized advice tailored to your circumstances. A mentor can also provide accountability and motivation, crucial components in achieving your financial goals. They can even offer insights into resources that are not widely known, adding to your overall learning experience and offering a personalized approach to financial literacy.

Finally, remember that financial literacy is not merely about accumulating knowledge; it's about applying that knowledge to your daily life. Regularly review your budget, track your spending, and adjust your financial strategies as needed. The resources outlined above are valuable tools, but their effectiveness depends on your commitment to actively using and applying the knowledge you gain. Building a strong financial foundation is a continuous process of learning, adapting, and refining your strategies. Embrace the challenge, and celebrate your progress along the way! The journey towards financial literacy may seem daunting at times, but with consistent effort and a willingness to learn, you will steadily build the skills and knowledge necessary to achieve your financial goals. The rewards of this sustained effort will far outweigh the initial investment of time and energy.

Developing a LongTerm Financial Plan

Developing a robust long-term financial plan is the cornerstone of achieving lasting financial success. It's not a one-time event, but rather a dynamic process of setting goals, strategizing, and adapting to life's changes. Think of it as your personalized financial roadmap, guiding you toward your desired financial future. This roadmap needs regular review and updates to remain relevant and effective, ensuring it aligns with your evolving circumstances and aspirations.

The first step in creating your long-term financial plan is to define your financial goals. What do you hope to achieve financially in the short-term (within the next 1-3 years), mid-term (3-5 years), and long-term (5+ years)? These goals might include buying a home, paying off student loans, saving for a down payment, funding your child's education, or securing a comfortable retirement. Be specific and quantify your goals whenever possible. Instead of saying "save for retirement," set a specific target, such as "accumulate $1 million by age 65." This specificity will provide you with a clear target to aim for and will allow you to develop strategies and milestones to measure your progress accurately.

Once you've defined your goals, you need to assess your current financial situation. This involves honestly evaluating your income, expenses, assets, and liabilities. This step requires diligent tracking of your income and expenses for at least a month, if not longer, to get a clear picture of your spending patterns. Create a detailed budget, categorizing your spending into essential needs (housing, food, transportation), wants (entertainment, dining out), and debt payments. Analyze this data to identify areas where you can reduce spending and increase savings. Tools like personal finance apps (Mint, Personal Capital, YNAB) can greatly assist in this process by automating the tracking and providing insightful visualizations of your spending habits.

Simultaneously, you need to evaluate your assets, such as savings accounts, investments, retirement accounts, and property. List their current values, and determine their potential for growth or

appreciation. Conversely, you also need to identify your liabilities, including outstanding loans (student loans, mortgages, credit card debts), and calculate their total outstanding balances and interest rates. This comprehensive assessment of your assets and liabilities will give you a clearer view of your net worth, providing the baseline for your long-term financial planning.

With a clear understanding of your goals and current financial state, you can now begin developing strategies to bridge the gap between where you are and where you want to be. This will involve

incorporating various investment strategies based on your risk tolerance, investment timeline, and financial goals. For instance, longer-term goals like retirement might allow for investments in higher-growth, higher-risk assets, such as stocks and mutual funds, while shorter-term goals might require more conservative

approaches like high-yield savings accounts or certificates of deposit.

Diversification is key to managing risk. Don't put all your eggs in one basket. Spread your investments across different asset classes to mitigate potential losses. The specific allocation will depend on your age, risk tolerance, and time horizon. A younger investor with a longer time horizon might allocate a larger portion of their

portfolio to stocks, while an older investor closer to retirement might prefer a more conservative allocation with a higher

proportion of bonds or fixed-income securities. This diversification should extend to different sectors within the stock market as well. Don't limit your investments to a single sector or industry; instead, diversify across different sectors to minimize the impact of potential industry downturns. Consider seeking guidance from a qualified financial advisor to create a portfolio allocation that aligns with your individual circumstances.

Consider the role of emergency funds. A robust emergency fund is essential for weathering unexpected financial setbacks, such as job loss, medical emergencies, or car repairs. Aim to build an emergency fund that can cover 3-6 months of your essential living expenses. This fund should be held in a readily accessible account, such as a high-yield savings account, allowing you to access the funds quickly in case of need. Don't let the desire to maximize investment returns compromise the necessity of maintaining a well-funded emergency fund. A sudden unexpected expense could derail your long-term financial goals if you lack adequate funds to handle it.

Once your emergency fund is established, you can begin

aggressively pursuing your other financial goals. Consider the various investment vehicles available, such as tax-advantaged retirement accounts (401(k), IRA, Roth IRA). These accounts offer significant tax benefits that can significantly boost your investment returns over time. Understanding the nuances of these accounts, such as contribution limits, tax implications, and withdrawal rules, is crucial for maximizing their benefits. Tax-advantaged investment vehicles should be a cornerstone of your long-term financial plan, significantly impacting your long-term financial security. Consider consulting a tax advisor or financial planner to understand the best strategy for utilizing these vehicles effectively.

Debt management is another crucial aspect of your long-term financial plan. High-interest debt, such as credit card debt, can significantly hinder your progress toward your financial goals.

Develop a strategy to pay off high-interest debt as quickly as

possible, perhaps through methods like the debt snowball or debt avalanche methods. The debt snowball method focuses on paying off the smallest debt first, building momentum and motivation, while the debt avalanche method focuses on paying off the highest-interest debt first to minimize the total interest paid. Either method can be effective, and the choice depends on your personal

preferences and financial circumstances. Once you have a plan for your debts, stick to it rigorously, ensuring you allocate sufficient funds to make significant payments each month.

Regularly review and adjust your financial plan. Life is dynamic, and your financial plan should adapt to your changing circumstances. Annually, or at least semi-annually, review your progress toward your financial goals, reassess your risk tolerance, and make necessary adjustments to your investment strategy.

Significant life events, such as marriage, having children, or

changing jobs, may require significant adjustments to your financial plan. Don't let your plan become stale; instead, treat it as a living document that evolves alongside your life. A flexible plan can handle unexpected changes and keep you on track towards your financial goals, even amidst significant life changes.

Finally, consider seeking professional guidance. A financial advisor can provide personalized advice and support, helping you navigate the complexities of financial planning. They can help you create a comprehensive plan that aligns with your individual goals, risk tolerance, and financial situation. While financial advisors charge fees for their services, the benefit of their expertise can be

invaluable in guiding your financial decisions and ensuring you're on a path to long-term financial success. However, be sure to research and vet any financial advisor before engaging their

services, ensuring their qualifications and experience align with your needs.

Creating a long-term financial plan is a journey, not a destination. It requires discipline, consistent effort, and a willingness to adapt. By following these steps, and consistently reviewing and updating your plan, you'll be well on your way to achieving your financial

aspirations and securing a financially secure future. Remember, the key is consistency and continuous learning. The more you learn and adapt, the stronger your financial foundation will become. Embrace the learning process, celebrate milestones, and remember that the journey itself is as rewarding as the destination.

Managing Unexpected Expenses

Unexpected expenses are the financial equivalent of a surprise pop quiz – they're unavoidable, stressful, and can completely derail your carefully crafted financial plan if you're not prepared. But unlike that pop quiz, you *can* prepare for these financial curveballs. The key is to anticipate the possibility of the unexpected and develop strategies to mitigate their impact. Think of it as building a

financial safety net, a cushion to soften the blow when life throws you a curveball.

The first line of defense against unexpected expenses is, of course, your emergency fund. We've already discussed the importance of building a 3-6 month emergency fund covering essential living expenses, but let's delve deeper into its practical application during a crisis. Imagine this: your car breaks down, requiring a $1,500 repair. Without an emergency fund, this could mean scrambling for credit cards, racking up high-interest debt, or even delaying crucial payments. With a robust emergency fund, however, you can calmly address the repair, avoiding the debt trap and maintaining the integrity of your long-term financial plan.

Beyond the car repair scenario, consider other unexpected expenses that might arise:

Medical emergencies: A sudden illness or injury can lead to

massive medical bills, even with health insurance. Deductibles, co-pays, and out-of-pocket maximums can quickly deplete your savings if you're not prepared. A well-funded emergency fund acts as a buffer, preventing you from falling into debt due to unforeseen medical costs. It also provides peace of mind, allowing you to focus on your health rather than the financial burden.

Job loss: The fear of job loss is a very real financial concern for many millennials. Unemployment benefits often don't fully replace your income, and finding a new job can take time. Your emergency fund is your lifeline during this period, providing a safety net to cover your essential expenses until you secure new employment.

This stability reduces stress and allows you to focus on your job search effectively. In fact, the stress reduction alone can improve your job search performance significantly. A prepared mind is a more productive mind.

Home repairs: Unexpected home repairs can be surprisingly costly.

A leaky roof, a malfunctioning appliance, or a burst pipe can all require significant financial investment. Having an emergency fund helps alleviate the stress associated with these events. You can address the problem promptly without sacrificing other financial commitments or resorting to high-interest debt.

Natural disasters: In many areas, the risk of natural disasters, such as hurricanes, floods, or wildfires, is significant. These events can cause extensive property damage and lead to significant financial losses. Having an emergency fund provides a safety net to help cover temporary relocation costs, property repairs, or the

replacement of essential belongings.

Unexpected travel expenses: Sometimes unforeseen circumstances require you to travel unexpectedly – perhaps a family emergency or a last-minute business trip. These trips can often come with

unplanned travel and accommodation expenses. Your emergency fund can help offset these unexpected costs, avoiding hasty

spending decisions.

It's crucial to understand that your emergency fund isn't just a safety net for catastrophic events. It's also a buffer for smaller, more frequent unexpected expenses that, while individually manageable, can cumulatively strain your budget. Think about unexpected car repairs, sudden veterinary bills for your pet, or even an unexpected increase in utility costs. These smaller expenses, if not handled properly, can lead to overspending on credit cards, contributing to accumulating debt and compromising your financial stability. Your emergency fund helps you handle these smaller surprises without resorting to debt.

Beyond your emergency fund, consider other safety nets:

Health insurance: Comprehensive health insurance is vital. While it doesn't eliminate all medical expenses, it significantly reduces the out-of-pocket costs associated with illness or injury.

Disability insurance: This insurance provides income replacement if you become unable to work due to illness or injury. It's a crucial safety net to protect your income and financial stability.

Life insurance: This protects your loved ones financially in case of your death. Depending on your circumstances, this could be crucial to provide financial support for dependents or pay off debts.

Homeowners or renters insurance: This protects your property from damage due to unforeseen events, such as fire, theft, or natural disasters. While it doesn't cover everything, it significantly reduces your financial exposure.

Auto insurance: This is legally mandated in most places, and crucial to protect yourself and your vehicle from financial losses due to accidents. Appropriate coverage protects you from

substantial financial burdens in case of an accident or theft.

These safety nets, combined with your emergency fund, create a robust financial defense system to protect you from unexpected expenses. But even with these precautions, unexpected situations can still arise. Here are some additional strategies to help navigate these challenging times:

Review your budget: When facing an unexpected expense, review your budget carefully to identify areas where you can temporarily reduce spending. This might involve cutting back on non-essential expenses, such as dining out or entertainment, to free up funds for the unexpected expense.

Negotiate with creditors: If you face a significant financial setback, don't hesitate to contact your creditors and explain your situation. Many creditors are willing to work with you to create a payment plan or temporarily reduce your payments. Open

communication can often prevent you from falling behind on your payments and incurring additional penalties.

Seek financial assistance: In some cases, seeking financial assistance might be necessary. This could involve applying for government assistance programs, seeking help from family or friends, or exploring options for debt consolidation or management. Don't be afraid to seek help when you need it – resources exist to help you navigate challenging financial times.

Re-evaluate your spending habits: After handling an unexpected expense, take the time to review your spending habits and identify potential areas of improvement. This process can help you better prepare for future unexpected expenses and develop healthier financial habits.

Unexpected expenses are a reality of life, but they don't have to be financially devastating. By proactively building a financial safety net, understanding your options, and acting responsibly, you can navigate these challenges and maintain your financial well-being.

Remember that financial preparedness is not just about having enough money; it's about having a plan and the mental resilience to handle whatever life throws your way. The feeling of being

prepared can significantly reduce stress levels and allow you to focus on resolving the unexpected problem more efficiently. It's a mindset shift, from panic to proactive problem-solving. And that's a valuable skill in any situation, financial or otherwise. Remember the importance of consistently reviewing and updating your

financial plan, including your emergency fund, to ensure it remains adequate for your evolving needs and circumstances. This ongoing attention allows your financial plan to act as a true safety net, providing the support and flexibility you need to manage life's inevitable surprises.

Coping with Job Loss or Unemployment

Job loss is a terrifying prospect, especially for millennials who may be navigating student loan debt, building a career, and establishing financial independence. The sudden absence of a regular paycheck can feel utterly overwhelming, triggering a cascade of anxieties about rent, bills, and the overall future. However, while job loss is undeniably stressful, it's not a financial death sentence. With a proactive approach and the right strategies, you can navigate this challenging period and emerge stronger on the other side.

The first step, and perhaps the most crucial, is to acknowledge your feelings. Don't suppress the shock, fear, or anger. Allow yourself to grieve the loss of your job. This isn't a sign of weakness; it's a healthy part of the process. Once you've allowed yourself to process these emotions, you can shift your focus to practical solutions.

Your emergency fund, as discussed previously, is your immediate lifeline. This isn't the time to feel guilty about using it; it's exactly what it's there for. Aim to utilize your emergency fund strategically, prioritizing essential expenses like rent, mortgage, utilities, and groceries. Create a detailed budget, meticulously tracking every expense to ensure you're stretching your resources as far as

possible. Consider downloading budgeting apps to assist with this process. They often offer helpful visualizations and insights into your spending habits.

Beyond your emergency fund, explore all available resources.

Unemployment benefits are your next line of defense. Each state has its own unemployment insurance system, so familiarize yourself with the application process and eligibility requirements in your state. Be prepared for some bureaucratic hurdles; the process might involve paperwork and waiting periods. Don't be discouraged; persistence pays off. In addition to unemployment benefits, explore potential assistance programs offered by your local government or non-profit organizations. Many cities and counties have assistance programs focused on helping people in times of unemployment.

Simultaneously, aggressively begin your job search. This requires a strategic and multifaceted approach. Update your resume and LinkedIn profile, highlighting your skills and accomplishments.

Tailor your resume and cover letter to each job application, showcasing how your skills directly relate to the specific position.

Don't limit yourself to online job boards; network with your contacts, attend industry events, and utilize your professional network for referrals.

Networking is often overlooked but is exceptionally valuable during a job search. Reach out to former colleagues, professors, mentors, and anyone else you've built a professional relationship with. Let them know you're looking for work and be specific about the types of roles you're targeting. You'd be surprised how often a conversation can lead to an opportunity. Don't be shy about asking for informational interviews, even if there isn't an open position at their company. These conversations can provide valuable insights into the job market and potentially uncover hidden opportunities.

Consider temporarily supplementing your income through freelancing or gig work. Platforms like Upwork, Fiverr, and TaskRabbit offer opportunities for short-term projects that can provide immediate financial relief. Even small amounts of income can ease the financial strain. While this isn't a long-term solution, it can buy you time and reduce stress while you search for a full-time job.

During this period, it's essential to prioritize your mental and physical health. Job loss can be incredibly stressful, leading to feelings of anxiety, depression, and isolation. Prioritize self-care activities such as exercise, meditation, spending time in nature, or engaging in hobbies you enjoy. Don't hesitate to reach out to friends, family, or mental health professionals for support. Your emotional well-being is just as critical as your financial well-being.

Lean on your support system; talking about your feelings can be incredibly therapeutic and help you navigate this challenging period.

Financial literacy plays a significant role in navigating job loss. Understanding your budget, accessing available resources, and strategizing your job search are all skills enhanced by a strong foundation in financial literacy. Use this time to strengthen your understanding of your finances. Review your spending habits, identify areas where you can cut back, and create a realistic budget for your anticipated income once you secure a new job.

Throughout this process, remember that you are not alone. Millions of people experience job loss, and many successfully navigate the challenges and emerge stronger. Maintain a positive mindset, focus on your strengths, and believe in your ability to find new employment. Job loss is a setback, not a failure. It's an opportunity to re-evaluate your career goals, acquire new skills, and perhaps even find a job that better aligns with your passions and values.

Consider upskilling or reskilling yourself. The job market is constantly evolving, and acquiring new skills can make you a more competitive candidate. Online courses, boot camps, and community college programs offer affordable options for enhancing your professional qualifications. Explore options that align with emerging industries or skills that are in high demand.

While focusing on immediate financial needs, don't neglect your long-term financial goals. If possible, maintain your contributions to retirement accounts, even if it means reducing the contribution amount. Consistency is key to long-term financial success. However, if doing so would compromise essential expenses, prioritize covering your immediate needs.

Open communication with your creditors is essential. If you anticipate difficulty meeting payment obligations, contact your lenders as soon as possible to explore options like forbearance or payment plans. Proactive communication can prevent late payment fees and damage to your credit score. Remember, most creditors would rather work with you than face non-payment.

Finally, celebrate your small victories along the way. Each job application submitted, each interview attended, and each networking connection made brings you closer to securing new employment. Acknowledge your progress and maintain a positive outlook. Remember, job loss is a temporary situation, and your resilience and adaptability will be your greatest strengths in overcoming this challenge. The journey may be challenging, but with proactive planning, resilience, and the support system you've cultivated, you will navigate through this and emerge financially stronger and more resourceful. Remember that seeking help isn't a sign of failure, it's a sign of strength and a smart financial strategy.

Many resources are available, and utilizing them is a key component to getting back on your feet.

Financial Planning During Major Life Changes

Marriage is a joyous occasion, a celebration of love and commitment. However, it also represents a significant financial shift. Suddenly, you're merging two households, two budgets, and potentially two very different financial philosophies. This transition necessitates careful planning and open communication to avoid future conflicts and ensure a solid financial foundation for your new life together.

Before the wedding bells chime, have a frank and honest discussion about your individual financial situations. Discuss your incomes, debts, savings, and spending habits. This isn't about judgment; it's about transparency and building a shared understanding of your collective financial landscape. Consider creating a joint spreadsheet to list all assets and liabilities, a clear picture of your starting point as a couple. This clarity will serve as the foundation for your joint financial journey.

One of the most crucial aspects of pre-marital financial planning is discussing long-term goals. Where do you see yourselves in five years? Ten years? Twenty years? Do you envision buying a home? Starting a family? Retiring early? These discussions will help align your financial strategies and ensure you're both working towards the same objectives. A shared vision is essential for navigating the financial complexities of marriage.

Debt is often a significant hurdle for couples starting their life together. Be transparent about any existing debts – student loans, credit card debt, or personal loans. Develop a strategy for managing and paying down this debt. Consider consolidating high-interest debts to reduce monthly payments and accelerate the repayment process. Prioritizing debt reduction can significantly improve your financial health as a couple and alleviate future stress.

Once married, decide how you'll manage your finances. Will you maintain separate accounts, open a joint account, or implement a hybrid approach? There's no one-size-fits-all solution. The key is to find a system that works for both of you, promotes transparency, and prevents misunderstandings. Clearly define who's responsible for paying which bills, ensuring a smooth and efficient process.

Budgeting as a couple requires collaboration and compromise.

Create a joint budget that reflects your shared expenses and individual needs. Categorize your expenses – housing, food, transportation, entertainment, and savings – and allocate funds accordingly. Regularly review and adjust your budget to

accommodate unexpected expenses or changes in income.

Budgeting apps can be incredibly helpful in managing joint finances.

Insurance is another critical aspect of financial planning for married couples. Review your health insurance coverage, life insurance policies, and other insurance needs. Make sure you have adequate coverage to protect yourselves and your future family. Consider updating beneficiaries on existing policies to reflect your marital status. This step protects your spouse in case of unforeseen

circumstances.

Estate planning is an essential but often overlooked aspect of marital financial planning. Create a will, designating beneficiaries for your assets. Consider establishing a power of attorney,

appointing someone to manage your finances if you become

incapacitated. This proactive approach ensures your wishes are carried out and protects your spouse's financial well-being. Having these legal documents in place provides peace of mind.

Having children represents another significant life change with far-reaching financial implications. The arrival of a child dramatically alters your spending patterns. Costs associated with childcare, education, healthcare, and other child-related expenses can quickly accumulate. Proactive financial planning is crucial to navigate these added costs effectively.

Before you even start trying for a baby, begin to strategize your finances. Revisit your budget and identify areas where you can adjust your spending to accommodate the anticipated increase in expenses. Consider adjusting savings goals to prioritize essential child-related expenses. Early planning provides you with ample time to adjust to the evolving financial landscape.

Childcare is often one of the largest expenses associated with raising a child. Research childcare options in your area and factor their costs into your budget. Consider exploring various options such as daycare, preschool, or in-home childcare, comparing costs and choosing the best solution based on your needs and financial situation. This early planning will help you anticipate your expenses accurately.

Healthcare expenses for children can be unpredictable. Make sure you have adequate health insurance coverage for your child.

Understand your health insurance plan's benefits and coverage limitations to avoid unexpected medical costs. Explore options to supplement your health insurance, such as health savings accounts (HSAs) or flexible spending accounts (FSAs). These tools can significantly reduce your out-of-pocket healthcare costs.

Education is another considerable long-term investment for parents. Start planning for your child's education early, even before they are born. Consider various options, such as public schools, private schools, or homeschooling, each with different cost implications. Explore college savings plans, such as 529 plans, to help fund your child's future education. These plans offer tax advantages and can significantly ease the financial burden of higher education.

Buying a home is a significant financial milestone for many millennials. It represents a substantial investment and comes with ongoing expenses, including mortgage payments, property taxes, insurance, and maintenance costs. Before you even start house hunting, take the time to evaluate your financial readiness. Assess your credit score, savings, and income to determine how much you can realistically afford.

Get pre-approved for a mortgage to understand your borrowing power. This step will help you narrow your house hunt and avoid wasting time looking at homes beyond your financial reach. It also provides you with a clear understanding of the monthly mortgage payments and other associated costs. Consider factors like down payment requirements, interest rates, and loan terms before finalizing a mortgage.

Once you've found a home, carefully review all the closing costs associated with the purchase. Closing costs can include appraisal fees, title insurance, escrow fees, and other charges. Ensure you have enough funds to cover these costs, which can often

significantly add to the total price of a home. Failing to plan for these expenses can derail your home-buying process.

After purchasing a home, plan for ongoing maintenance expenses.

Regular maintenance, such as repairs and upgrades, can help protect your investment and keep your home in good condition. Create a home maintenance budget to account for these costs and avoid unexpected financial burdens. Setting aside funds specifically for this purpose can significantly aid in managing homeownership effectively.

Major life changes, like marriage, having children, and buying a home, necessitate a proactive and flexible approach to financial planning. Open communication, shared goals, and adaptable budgeting are critical to navigating these transitions smoothly. Don't be afraid to adjust your plans as circumstances evolve; life is full of unexpected twists and turns. By remaining adaptable, maintaining open communication, and prioritizing financial education, you can build a secure financial future, despite life's challenges. Remember, seeking professional financial advice is always a valuable option, especially during major life changes.

Seeking Professional Financial Advice

Seeking professional financial advice is often the wisest investment you can make, especially during periods of significant life change.

While diligent self-education and careful planning are crucial, a seasoned financial advisor can provide invaluable expertise,

objectivity, and a personalized roadmap tailored to your unique circumstances. They can help navigate the complexities of financial planning, offering insights you might miss while trying to manage it all alone. This is particularly true during periods like marriage, parenthood, or homeownership, when financial responsibilities multiply and the stakes are high.

One of the primary benefits of engaging a financial advisor is the access to personalized financial planning. Generic advice found online or in books can only offer a generalized approach. A

financial advisor will take the time to understand your specific goals, risk tolerance, and financial situation – your income, assets, liabilities, and spending habits. They'll then use this information to create a customized plan designed to maximize your wealth and secure your financial future. This personalized approach ensures your strategy is aligned with your aspirations, not just a generic template. For example, if you're aiming for early retirement, your advisor will develop a strategy that prioritizes aggressive savings and investment, potentially involving higher-risk investments. On the other hand, someone closer to retirement might require a more conservative strategy emphasizing preservation of capital and income generation.

Beyond personalized planning, financial advisors offer valuable expertise in investment management. Investing your money wisely is crucial for building wealth, but navigating the complexities of the market can be overwhelming for the average person. A financial advisor possesses in-depth knowledge of various investment options, including stocks, bonds, mutual funds, real estate, and alternative investments. They can help you diversify your portfolio, reducing your overall risk and maximizing your return. This expertise is particularly important during volatile market conditions, where amateur investors might panic sell or make poor decisions based on emotion rather than sound financial strategy. They can also help you understand complex financial instruments and strategies, such as tax-loss harvesting, asset allocation, and estate planning, that can significantly impact your financial health.

Moreover, a financial advisor can help you develop and implement a comprehensive debt management strategy. High-interest debt can severely hamper your financial progress, and managing multiple debts can become incredibly complex. A financial advisor can assist in analyzing your debt, developing a repayment plan, and negotiating with creditors to reduce interest rates or monthly payments. They can advise on debt consolidation strategies, helping you streamline your payments and potentially save money on interest. For instance, they might recommend refinancing high-interest credit card debt into a lower-interest personal loan or exploring debt management programs offered by credit counseling agencies. This structured approach to debt management can significantly improve your financial health and free up resources for other financial goals.

Another crucial area where financial advisors provide significant value is retirement planning. Retirement might seem distant, but planning for it early is crucial to ensure a comfortable and secure financial future. A financial advisor will help you determine your retirement needs, taking into account factors such as your desired lifestyle, expected expenses, and anticipated longevity. They can then create a comprehensive retirement plan, outlining strategies for saving, investing, and managing your retirement funds. They'll also help you understand various retirement accounts, such as 401(k)s, IRAs, and Roth IRAs, and choose the options best suited to your needs. They can assist with optimizing your contributions to maximize tax advantages and projected retirement income.

Beyond retirement and debt management, financial advisors can offer crucial guidance in estate planning. Estate planning ensures your assets are distributed according to your wishes, protecting your loved ones from unnecessary financial burdens and potential legal disputes after your death. A financial advisor can help you create a comprehensive estate plan, including a will, trust, power of attorney, and healthcare directive. They'll guide you through complex legal and tax implications, helping you minimize estate taxes and ensure a smooth transfer of your assets. This proactive approach ensures your legacy is handled with care and provides peace of mind for both you and your family.

Choosing the right financial advisor is a crucial step in the process.

It's important to find someone you trust, someone whose values align with yours, and someone who has a proven track record of success. Start by researching different advisors in your area or online. Look for advisors with relevant certifications, such as a Certified Financial Planner (CFP) designation. This designation signifies that the advisor has met specific education and experience requirements, adhering to a strict code of ethics. Check their

credentials with the relevant regulatory bodies to ensure they are legitimate and licensed to practice.

When interviewing potential advisors, ask about their fees and services. Financial advisors typically charge fees based on assets under management (AUM), hourly rates, or a combination of both. Understand exactly how they are compensated and what services are included in their fees. Don't hesitate to ask for references and testimonials from past clients. Speaking to previous clients can provide valuable insights into their experience working with the advisor, allowing you to gauge their professionalism,

responsiveness, and overall effectiveness.

Assessing the value of professional financial advice often comes down to comparing the cost of the services against the potential benefits. The fees you pay should be viewed as an investment in your financial future. A skilled advisor can help you avoid costly mistakes, optimize your investments, and develop a strategic plan that maximizes your financial well-being. Think of it as paying for expertise and peace of mind, knowing your financial future is in capable hands. While you might find free resources online, they lack the personalized touch and strategic planning that a

professional financial advisor can offer.

Finally, remember that the relationship with your financial advisor should be ongoing. Your financial needs and goals will change over time. Regular meetings and reviews will allow your advisor to adjust your plan as needed, ensuring it remains aligned with your evolving circumstances. This proactive approach helps you stay on track, adapt to unexpected challenges, and achieve your long-term financial goals. Choosing to engage a professional financial advisor isn't just about managing money; it's about securing your financial future and empowering yourself to make informed decisions. It's about achieving financial freedom and peace of mind, allowing you to focus on the things that truly matter in life.

Building a Support System

Building a strong support system is often overlooked in personal finance discussions, yet it's a crucial element in navigating life's financial hurdles. While professional advice is invaluable, the emotional and practical support from a trusted network can be equally significant, providing a buffer against stress and offering different perspectives during challenging times. Think of it as having your own financial "cheerleading squad," offering

encouragement and a sounding board when you need it most.

The benefits of sharing your financial journey with others are numerous. First, it can foster accountability. When you share your goals – whether it's saving for a down payment, paying off debt, or investing for retirement – with someone you trust, you're more likely to stick to your plan. This accountability partner can check in on your progress, offer encouragement when you falter, and help you stay motivated. It's similar to joining a fitness challenge with a friend; the shared commitment boosts adherence. Imagine sharing your goal of saving $10,000 for a down payment with a close friend. Regular check-ins keep you both motivated, and you can celebrate milestones together. The shared journey transforms what could be a solitary and potentially daunting task into a

collaborative effort.

Secondly, a support system offers a sounding board for ideas and concerns. Financial decisions are rarely simple, and bouncing ideas off trusted individuals can bring clarity and help you avoid costly mistakes. A fresh perspective from a friend or family member might illuminate an overlooked risk or reveal a more efficient approach.

For example, if you're considering a major purchase like a car, discussing your plans with a trusted advisor who is financially savvy could help you analyze potential pitfalls, such as financing options and hidden fees. Their feedback might prevent an impulsive decision with significant long-term repercussions. They may point out cheaper alternatives or suggest strategies to secure a better loan.

The nature of this support can vary. It could be a close friend who has successfully navigated similar financial challenges, a family member who is financially responsible and provides insightful advice, or a mentor who has achieved significant financial success.

Their experience can provide invaluable lessons and perspective, offering a roadmap to avoid common pitfalls. Mentors, in

particular, can share their own hard-earned wisdom, saving you years of trial and error. They offer not just advice, but also guidance in building healthy financial habits and developing the resilience needed to overcome setbacks.

Consider the scenario of someone struggling with high-interest debt.

Sharing this with a supportive friend or mentor can create an environment where vulnerability is safe and solutions are explored collaboratively. The mentor might suggest specific debt reduction strategies, like the snowball or avalanche method, or introduce them to resources like credit counseling agencies. The friend's empathetic ear and consistent encouragement could provide the emotional support needed to persevere through the arduous process of debt repayment. This combined approach – practical strategies and emotional encouragement – significantly improves the chances of success.

Choosing your support system wisely is also vital. While close family members are often the first point of contact, it's essential to select individuals whose advice aligns with your values and

financial goals. Avoid seeking advice from individuals whose

financial habits you wouldn't emulate. Your support network should be composed of individuals who encourage responsible financial decisions and understand your long-term aspirations. You want individuals who celebrate your successes and offer constructive feedback during setbacks, not those who might enable poor

financial choices or criticize your efforts.

Another crucial aspect of building a supportive network is

maintaining open and honest communication. Avoid hiding your financial struggles or downplaying your challenges. Transparency fosters trust and enables your support network to offer relevant and timely assistance. It's much easier to tackle financial challenges when you have others who are aware of your circumstances and willing to offer their support. Imagine sharing the stress of an unexpected job loss with a close friend or family member. Their empathy and practical help, like assistance with budgeting or finding alternative resources, would be invaluable.

The power of a supportive network extends beyond immediate financial challenges. It is also essential for long-term financial planning and goal setting. Sharing your financial goals – be it buying a house, saving for retirement, or starting a business – with a supportive group can enhance your commitment and resilience.

Regular discussions regarding savings strategies, investment options, and financial planning can prevent you from making impulsive decisions that could have long-term consequences. This shared journey creates a positive reinforcement loop, supporting your financial wellbeing and promoting lasting change.

This doesn't mean blindly accepting every piece of advice; it's about gaining multiple perspectives and leveraging the collective wisdom of your chosen support network. After discussing your financial plans and concerns with several people, you can synthesize this information, making more informed decisions based on a broader understanding of your options. This approach encourages critical thinking and empowers you to take ownership of your financial future. Remember to carefully weigh the advice you receive,

filtering it through your own circumstances and long-term goals.

However, it's equally important to establish boundaries within your support system. While sharing your financial struggles is beneficial, it's also crucial to protect your privacy and avoid oversharing

sensitive information. Choose your confidantes carefully, ensuring they understand the importance of discretion and respecting your boundaries. Financial discussions should always feel safe and

empowering, not leading to feelings of judgment or increased stress. Creating a space where vulnerability is welcome, but not exploited, is vital to the success of a supportive financial network.

Finally, remember that building a strong support system is an ongoing process. Your network might evolve over time as your circumstances and financial goals change. Maintain open

communication with your support system, keeping them updated on your progress and seeking their guidance when needed. Don't hesitate to reach out to your network even during periods of relative financial stability, strengthening your bonds and ensuring they are readily available during periods of greater need.

Cultivating a strong and supportive network of friends, family, or mentors is as important as seeking professional financial advice, providing an invaluable emotional and practical support system to navigate the complexities of life's financial challenges. This holistic approach to financial well-being is essential for achieving long-term financial success and overall contentment. It is about creating a community that celebrates your wins and offers comfort and

guidance during difficult times, a collaborative journey towards a secure and fulfilling financial future.

Defining Financial Independence

Defining financial independence isn't about hitting a specific number in your bank account; it's about achieving a state of being where your passive income surpasses your expenses. It's the freedom to choose how you spend your time and resources, without the constant pressure of needing to work just to cover basic living costs. This isn't necessarily about accumulating vast wealth; it's about creating a sustainable financial ecosystem that supports your lifestyle and aspirations. Think of it as building a sturdy financial foundation that can withstand unexpected life events, allowing you to pursue opportunities and experiences without the looming threat of financial insecurity.

The path to financial independence is rarely linear. It's a journey shaped by individual circumstances, financial goals, and risk tolerance. For some, it might involve diligently saving and investing over several decades, patiently watching their portfolio grow. Others might pursue more aggressive strategies, focusing on high-growth investments with a higher level of risk. Some might find financial independence through entrepreneurship, building a business that generates substantial passive income streams. There is no "one-size-fits-all" approach. The key is to identify a strategy that aligns with your personal circumstances, risk profile, and long-term aspirations.

A crucial element in defining your path to financial independence is understanding your spending habits. Before you can start planning for financial freedom, you need to develop a realistic understanding of where your money goes. Tracking your expenses for a few months, using budgeting apps or spreadsheets, can reveal surprising patterns. You might discover you're spending more on entertainment or dining out than you initially thought. This awareness is the foundation of effective budgeting. Once you have a grasp of your spending, you can identify areas where you can reduce expenses and redirect those funds towards savings and investments.

Budgeting isn't about deprivation; it's about making conscious choices about how you allocate your resources. It's about prioritizing your financial goals and aligning your spending with your values. Consider creating a detailed budget that categorizes your expenses, clearly outlining your essential needs and discretionary spending. This visual representation of your financial picture can help you identify areas for improvement. For instance, you might choose to reduce subscription services you rarely use or find cheaper alternatives for groceries. The goal isn't to eliminate all discretionary spending but to consciously choose where you allocate your funds.

Beyond budgeting, investing plays a pivotal role in achieving financial independence. Investing allows your money to work for you, generating passive income that grows over time. Depending on your risk tolerance and investment timeline, you can choose from a range of investment options, such as stocks, bonds, mutual funds, real estate, and index funds. It's essential to conduct thorough research and potentially seek professional advice before making any significant investment decisions. Diversification is key to mitigating risk; spreading your investments across different asset classes helps to protect your portfolio against market fluctuations.

Education is another crucial component of achieving financial independence. It's not just about formal education, but also about continuous learning and seeking knowledge. The world of personal finance is constantly evolving, and staying updated on financial trends and investment strategies is paramount. There are numerous resources available, from personal finance books and online courses to financial podcasts and webinars. These resources can provide valuable insights and help you make informed financial decisions. Investing time in learning about financial literacy is an investment in your future financial wellbeing.

The timeline for achieving financial independence varies widely. It's heavily influenced by factors such as income, expenses, investment returns, and life circumstances. For some, it might take several decades of diligent saving and investing; for others, it might be achieved sooner, depending on their career trajectory, financial decisions, and risk tolerance. It's crucial to establish realistic

expectations and avoid comparing your journey to others'. Focus on your own pace and progress, celebrating milestones along the way, rather than fixating on an arbitrary timeframe.

Debt management is another significant factor to consider. High-interest debt, such as credit card debt, can severely hamper your progress toward financial independence. Creating a plan to eliminate or manage high-interest debt strategically is essential. Methods such as the debt snowball or avalanche method can help you prioritize your debt repayment, accelerating your journey towards financial freedom. Negotiating lower interest rates with lenders or exploring debt consolidation options can also significantly reduce your debt burden and free up more money for saving and investing.

Beyond financial strategies, developing good financial habits is crucial. This involves making conscious choices about your spending, saving, and investing habits, embedding financial discipline into your daily life. It's about cultivating a mindful approach to money, where every decision is made with intention and awareness. This mindful financial practice can help you build a strong foundation for long-term financial success. Avoid impulsive spending and prioritize building a solid emergency fund.

The psychological aspect of achieving financial independence is often overlooked. The journey to financial freedom can be mentally challenging, requiring patience, discipline, and resilience. The ability to delay gratification, make sacrifices in the short term for long-term gains, and stay motivated during periods of setbacks is essential. Celebrating milestones, no matter how small, and maintaining a positive attitude can significantly boost morale and keep you motivated along the way.

Building a strong support system is also vital. Having a network of trusted friends, family, or mentors who can offer advice, encouragement, and accountability can significantly enhance your chances of success. They can provide perspective during difficult times, offer encouragement when you feel discouraged, and help you stay on track towards your financial goals. Openly discussing your financial aspirations and challenges with your support network can foster accountability and make the journey less daunting.

In conclusion, financial independence is a multifaceted concept that involves a combination of effective financial planning, strategic investing, disciplined saving, and a positive mindset. It's a journey, not a destination, requiring commitment, resilience, and a clear understanding of your personal financial goals. By combining practical financial strategies with a supportive network and a positive attitude, you can significantly increase your chances of achieving financial freedom and living the life you desire.

Remember, the journey is unique to you; focus on your own progress and celebrate every step towards financial independence.

Measuring Your Progress Towards Financial Freedom

Measuring your progress towards financial independence isn't about obsessively checking your bank account daily; it's about establishing a system for tracking your key metrics and celebrating your wins along the way. Think of it as charting a course across an ocean –you need regular navigation to ensure you're on track, and acknowledging each milestone keeps you motivated and focused.

This section will provide you with the tools and techniques to effectively track your progress, ensuring your financial journey remains exciting and rewarding.

First, let's establish some key metrics. These aren't rigid rules, but flexible guides that you can tailor to your specific circumstances and goals. A crucial starting point is your **net worth** . This is the difference between your assets (what you own) and your liabilities (what you owe). Assets include things like cash, savings, investments, property, and even valuable possessions. Liabilities encompass debt like mortgages, loans, and credit card balances. Tracking your net worth regularly, perhaps monthly or quarterly, gives you a clear picture of your overall financial health. You can use a simple spreadsheet or a dedicated personal finance app to calculate and monitor your net worth. Aim to see consistent growth in this figure over time.

Beyond net worth, monitoring your **savings rate** is critical. This represents the percentage of your income that you're successfully saving each month or year. A high savings rate is a strong indicator that you're on track to achieve financial independence. Calculating your savings rate involves dividing your total savings by your gross income. For instance, if you saved $5,000 and earned $50,000 in a year, your savings rate is 10%. Ideally, you'll aim for a savings rate significantly higher than the average, perhaps 20%, 30%, or even higher, depending on your financial goals and lifestyle. Keep in mind that your savings rate might fluctuate from month to month or year to year depending on unexpected expenses or income changes. The key is to maintain a generally upward trend over the long term.

Another valuable metric is your **passive income** . As you progress towards financial independence, a growing stream of passive income is crucial. This income is generated without requiring active work, such as rental income from real estate, dividends from stocks, interest from savings accounts, or royalties from creative works.

Track your passive income separately from your earned income. Watch how this passive income stream grows over time, eventually aiming for it to cover a significant portion, and ultimately all, of your expenses. This is a crucial milestone on your journey to financial freedom.

Furthermore, keep a close eye on your **debt-to-income ratio (DTI)** . This metric illustrates the proportion of your monthly income dedicated to debt payments. A low DTI indicates a healthier financial situation, showing that you're not overburdened with debt. A high DTI, on the other hand, signifies that a large portion of your income is consumed by debt payments, possibly hindering your progress towards financial independence. Calculate this ratio by dividing your total monthly debt payments by your gross monthly income. Strive to reduce this ratio over time by strategically paying down debt.

Finally, don't underestimate the power of regularly reviewing your **budget** . While we've already discussed budgeting, consistent review is paramount. Your financial situation is dynamic; your income, expenses, and financial goals might change over time. Regularly reviewing your budget, perhaps monthly, allows you to adjust your spending habits, identify areas for improvement, and ensure your budget continues to support your financial objectives. This constant monitoring ensures you stay adaptable and proactive in managing your finances.

Beyond these key metrics, consider establishing personal benchmarks. These are milestones specific to your unique financial journey. Perhaps it's paying off a significant debt, reaching a certain net worth, or generating a specific amount of passive income. Set realistic, yet challenging, goals. Celebrate each achievement; these are significant victories along the way. Remember, financial

independence is a marathon, not a sprint. Acknowledging your progress keeps you motivated and engaged throughout the entire journey.

To make tracking your progress more visual and engaging, consider using a variety of tools and techniques. Spreadsheets are an

excellent starting point, allowing you to organize your financial data and visually track your metrics over time. Dedicated personal finance apps can automate much of the data entry and provide insightful visualizations of your progress. Some apps even offer features to set financial goals and monitor progress against those targets.

Visual representations of your progress are invaluable. Creating charts and graphs from your financial data can make your journey more tangible and inspiring. See your net worth climb, your savings rate increase, and your passive income grow. This visual

representation can be a powerful motivator, providing a clear illustration of your success. Consider sharing your progress with a trusted friend or mentor for added accountability and support.

Their encouragement and feedback can be incredibly valuable in maintaining your momentum.

Don't let setbacks discourage you. Everyone experiences financial bumps along the way. Unexpected expenses, job loss, or market fluctuations can impact your progress. The key is to remain

resilient, adapt to changing circumstances, and adjust your

strategies as needed. Don't dwell on setbacks; analyze what

happened, learn from the experience, and re-focus on your overall financial goals. Celebrate even small victories; these moments help you stay positive and motivated.

Remember, the journey to financial freedom is deeply personal. What works for one person might not work for another. Experiment with different tracking methods and find what best suits your personality and preferences. The most important aspect is to

consistently monitor your progress, celebrate your achievements, and stay committed to your long-term financial goals. Your consistent effort and dedication will ultimately lead you to the financial freedom you desire.

Finally, integrate this progress tracking into your lifestyle. Make it a

regular part of your financial routine. Schedule time each month or quarter to review your progress, analyze your performance against your benchmarks, and adjust your strategies as needed. This

consistent monitoring is crucial in ensuring you stay on track and achieve your desired financial independence. Don't just passively wait for financial freedom to happen; actively pursue it by

diligently monitoring your progress and celebrating every milestone along the way. This proactive approach will significantly enhance your chances of success. This mindful engagement with your

financial progress transforms the journey from a daunting task into an empowering and rewarding experience. Celebrate the journey; enjoy the process; you're building a better future for yourself.

Maintaining Financial Health and Wellness

Maintaining your financial well-being isn't a destination; it's an ongoing journey. Achieving financial independence is a significant milestone, but sustaining that freedom requires consistent effort and proactive management. This section focuses on the crucial strategies for maintaining long-term financial health, ensuring your hard-earned financial freedom endures.

One of the most critical aspects of maintaining financial wellness is the ongoing refinement of your budget. While we've discussed creating a budget, remember it's not a static document carved in stone. Life changes, expenses fluctuate, and income might shift.

Regularly reviewing and adjusting your budget is paramount to staying on top of your finances. Consider reviewing your budget monthly, or at least quarterly, to ensure it accurately reflects your current financial situation. This isn't about rigid adherence; it's about adapting to life's inevitable changes. Perhaps you received a raise, necessitating an adjustment to your savings goals or allowing for increased discretionary spending. Maybe unexpected home repairs popped up, necessitating a temporary shift in your spending priorities. The key is flexibility and responsiveness. Regularly reviewing your budget allows you to identify areas where you're overspending, pinpoint areas for potential savings, and recalibrate your financial plan to align with your evolving needs. Tools like budgeting apps can automate much of this process, making it less daunting and more manageable.

Beyond budgeting, consistent monitoring of your investments is crucial. This isn't about daily market fluctuations; it's about a

regular assessment of your investment portfolio's performance against your long-term goals. Review your investments at least annually, and more frequently if you're actively trading or if

significant market events occur. This involves evaluating your asset allocation, assessing the performance of individual investments, and adjusting your strategy as needed. Are your investments still aligned with your risk tolerance and time horizon? Do you need to

rebalance your portfolio to maintain your desired asset allocation? Are you on track to achieve your long-term financial goals, such as retirement or early financial freedom? This regular review allows you to identify potential issues early, make necessary adjustments, and ensure your investments remain aligned with your overall financial plan. Remember, professional financial advice can be invaluable, particularly during times of uncertainty or when making significant investment decisions.

Regular review of your overall financial plan is as crucial as

monitoring your budget and investments. Your financial plan isn't a one-time creation; it's a living document that requires periodic updates and adjustments. Life events, such as marriage, the birth of a child, or a career change, can significantly impact your financial goals and strategies. Regularly reviewing your financial plan, at least annually, allows you to assess your progress against your goals, evaluate the effectiveness of your strategies, and make necessary changes to ensure you stay on track. This review process should encompass all aspects of your financial life, from your budget and investments to your debt management and estate planning. Consider documenting your financial plan, outlining your short-term and long-term goals, and detailing the strategies you're employing to achieve those goals. This documentation provides a valuable roadmap for your financial journey and serves as a

reminder of your aspirations.

Continuous learning and adaptation are integral to maintaining long-term financial health. The financial landscape is constantly evolving, with new investment opportunities, economic shifts, and technological advancements impacting the way we manage our money. Staying informed about these changes is crucial to making sound financial decisions. This involves reading financial news, staying updated on economic trends, and continuously educating yourself about various financial products and services. Consider subscribing to reputable financial publications, attending financial literacy workshops, or enrolling in online courses to enhance your financial knowledge. The goal isn't to become a financial expert overnight, but to cultivate a consistent habit of learning and adapting to the ever-changing financial environment. This

commitment to continuous learning empowers you to make

informed decisions, adjust your strategies as needed, and navigate unexpected financial challenges with confidence. Remember, financial literacy is an ongoing process; it's a commitment to continuous improvement.

Building a strong financial foundation requires resilience and the ability to adapt to unforeseen circumstances. Unexpected events, such as job loss, medical emergencies, or economic downturns, can significantly impact even the most meticulously crafted financial plans. Developing resilience involves maintaining an emergency fund, diversifying your investments, and cultivating a flexible mindset. An emergency fund serves as a safety net during unexpected financial challenges, allowing you to weather the storm without derailing your long-term financial goals. Diversification of investments mitigates risk by spreading your assets across various asset classes, reducing the impact of any single investment's underperformance. A flexible mindset allows you to adapt to unforeseen circumstances, adjusting your plans as needed without losing sight of your long-term financial objectives. Remember, setbacks are inevitable; it's your response that shapes your long-term financial success. Analyze your situation, adapt your strategies, and continue moving forward.

Maintaining financial health and wellness goes beyond simply accumulating wealth; it encompasses a holistic approach to your financial life. This involves regularly reviewing your budget and investments, adapting to changing circumstances, and consistently learning and growing. It's about building a sustainable financial foundation that supports your lifestyle and helps you achieve your long-term goals. This mindful engagement with your finances isn't simply about accumulating money; it's about creating a secure and fulfilling financial future for yourself. It's about peace of mind, knowing you're prepared for life's unexpected challenges.

Consider seeking professional advice. While this guide provides valuable insights, every individual's financial situation is unique. A financial advisor can provide personalized guidance based on your specific circumstances, goals, and risk tolerance. They can help you develop a comprehensive financial plan, manage your investments, and navigate complex financial issues. Remember, seeking

professional help doesn't signify a lack of knowledge or ability; it's a strategic investment in your financial future. An experienced advisor can provide unbiased perspectives, help you avoid costly mistakes, and ultimately optimize your financial trajectory.

Finally, remember that your financial journey is a marathon, not a sprint. There will be ups and downs, unexpected challenges, and moments of doubt. The key is to maintain a long-term perspective, celebrate your achievements along the way, and stay committed to your financial goals. Celebrate those small wins – paying off a debt, hitting a savings target, or even simply sticking to your budget for a month. These moments reinforce your commitment and keep you motivated throughout the journey. Maintain a positive mindset, focusing on your progress and the ultimate rewards of financial freedom. This commitment to long-term financial health ensures your financial well-being and provides a strong foundation for a secure and fulfilling future. Remember, the ultimate goal isn't just financial freedom; it's financial wellness – a state of being where you are not only financially secure but also emotionally and

mentally at ease with your financial situation. That's the true

definition of achieving financial independence and living the life you've always dreamed of.

Giving Back and Building a Legacy

Having achieved financial freedom, a profound sense of

accomplishment washes over you. But true fulfillment often extends beyond personal enrichment. It encompasses a desire to contribute meaningfully to the world around you and to secure the future of those you care about. This is where the concepts of giving back and building a legacy come into play, adding another layer of depth and meaning to your financial journey.

Philanthropy, often perceived as the exclusive domain of the ultra-wealthy, is actually accessible to everyone, regardless of their income level. It's not about writing a six-figure check to a major charity; it's about aligning your values with your actions and

contributing in ways that resonate with you. This could involve volunteering your time at a local soup kitchen, mentoring

underprivileged youth, donating to a cause you're passionate about, or simply offering a helping hand to a neighbor in need. The

impact, both on the recipient and on yourself, is immeasurable.

The act of giving back offers more than just altruistic satisfaction. Studies have consistently shown that charitable giving is associated with increased happiness and well-being. The simple act of helping others triggers the release of endorphins, creating a positive

feedback loop that enhances your emotional and mental health. This isn't simply about feeling good; it's about fostering a sense of purpose and connection to something larger than yourself. When you actively participate in your community, you build stronger relationships, foster a sense of belonging, and create a more positive social environment.

Furthermore, strategic philanthropy can also have unexpected financial benefits. Many charitable donations are tax-deductible, offering a tangible financial incentive while also aligning your values with your financial strategy. This is not about using charity as a tax avoidance scheme; rather, it's about maximizing the impact of your contributions. Carefully researching charities and

understanding their financial transparency and impact will ensure your donations are used effectively and efficiently. Don't just look at the bottom line; understand the organization's mission, its impact on the community, and how your contribution will directly affect its work.

Beyond direct charitable contributions, consider exploring other avenues of giving back. This could involve supporting socially responsible businesses, investing in companies with strong ethical practices, or engaging in impact investing – investing in ventures that generate both financial returns and positive social or

environmental impact. Impact investing is a growing trend that allows individuals to align their investment portfolio with their values, creating a win-win situation where your money generates both profits and positive change.

Building a legacy extends beyond financial provision; it involves shaping a lasting impact on future generations. This is about more than just leaving a large inheritance; it's about passing on values, knowledge, and a commitment to social responsibility. For many, this involves establishing a trust fund or other estate-planning mechanisms to ensure the long-term financial security of loved ones. This requires careful planning and consultation with financial and legal professionals to ensure your wishes are carried out

effectively and efficiently, minimizing potential tax implications and family disputes.

A well-structured estate plan provides more than financial security; it provides peace of mind, knowing that your family is protected and your assets are managed according to your wishes. This process may involve creating a will, establishing trusts, setting up life insurance policies, and designating beneficiaries for various

accounts. Engaging a qualified estate attorney and financial advisor is crucial in this process, ensuring the plan is legally sound, tax-efficient, and aligned with your personal goals.

However, building a legacy is not solely about financial resources; it's also about sharing knowledge, values, and life experiences. This could involve mentoring younger generations, sharing your

financial expertise with family members, or documenting your life experiences and lessons learned. These intangible legacies can be as powerful, if not more so, than any financial inheritance. Consider leaving behind a written account of your life's journey, including the financial challenges you faced and the strategies you employed to overcome them. This can serve as an invaluable resource for your family, providing guidance and inspiration for future generations.

Moreover, your legacy extends beyond your immediate family. It encompasses the impact you have on your community and the world at large. Consider your contributions to your profession, your involvement in community organizations, and the positive impact you've had on the lives of others. These contributions may not be immediately quantifiable in monetary terms, but they represent a significant and lasting legacy. You can actively contribute to your legacy by mentoring colleagues, volunteering in your field of expertise, or becoming involved in community leadership roles.

Consider the impact of your lifestyle choices on your legacy.

Promoting sustainable practices, supporting environmentally responsible businesses, and minimizing your carbon footprint contribute to a positive environmental legacy. Future generations will inherit the consequences of our current actions; therefore, making conscious choices today ensures a better future for them. This demonstrates responsible stewardship of the planet and sets a positive example for future generations.

Furthermore, your digital legacy should also be considered. In today's digital age, our online presence persists long after we are gone. Managing your digital footprint – reviewing your social media accounts, organizing digital files, and designating access to important online accounts – is a crucial aspect of responsible estate planning. This ensures the privacy and security of your digital assets, protecting your personal information and allowing loved ones access to important documents and information.

Building a legacy is a continuous process, not a one-time event. It's about consistently making choices aligned with your values and contributing positively to the world around you. It's a journey of growth, learning, and giving back, encompassing both financial and intangible contributions. Your legacy is a testament to your life's work and a lasting gift to future generations. It's about the mark you leave on the world, both big and small, and the positive impact you have on the lives of others. It's a testament to your life's

journey, the challenges overcome, and the wisdom shared. By incorporating philanthropy and legacy building into your long-term financial plan, you create a richer, more fulfilling life, extending your impact far beyond your own lifetime. And that's the true measure of lasting wealth – a wealth of purpose, contribution, and meaningful connections that resonate through generations. It's about leaving a legacy that inspires, empowers, and strengthens the fabric of society. The culmination of your financial journey should not just be about personal financial freedom, but a holistic freedom that includes purpose, contribution, and a lasting positive impact on the world around you.

The Ongoing Journey to Financial Success

The journey to financial freedom isn't a sprint; it's a marathon, and even after crossing the finish line, the race continues in a new and equally rewarding way. Achieving financial independence is a monumental accomplishment, a testament to your discipline, foresight, and hard work. But it's not the end; it's merely a

transformative milestone, opening doors to new opportunities and perspectives. The ongoing journey involves navigating new

challenges, embracing continuous learning, and adapting to the ever-evolving economic landscape.

One of the key aspects of this ongoing journey is the cultivation of a growth mindset. Financial success isn't static; it's dynamic. The strategies and techniques that served you well in your early years may need adjustments as your circumstances change. The economy fluctuates, interest rates shift, and new investment opportunities emerge. Remaining adaptable and open to learning new skills and strategies is essential to maintaining your financial momentum and maximizing your potential.

This requires a commitment to ongoing education. The world of personal finance is constantly evolving, with new technologies, regulations, and investment vehicles appearing regularly. Staying informed is crucial to making sound financial decisions and

avoiding costly mistakes. Consider regularly reading financial publications, attending workshops and seminars, or even pursuing advanced certifications to enhance your financial literacy.

Numerous online resources and educational platforms offer valuable information on diverse aspects of personal finance, ranging from budgeting and investing to tax planning and estate management.

Moreover, seeking advice from trusted financial professionals can be invaluable. A financial advisor can offer personalized guidance tailored to your specific circumstances, providing objective insights and helping you navigate complex financial matters. They can help you create and maintain a comprehensive financial plan, monitor your progress, and make adjustments as needed. Remember,

seeking professional guidance isn't a sign of weakness; it's a sign of wisdom and a commitment to making informed choices.

Beyond formal education, continuous learning involves staying updated on current events and their impact on the economy.

Understanding macroeconomic trends, geopolitical events, and regulatory changes can inform your investment decisions and help you navigate economic uncertainties. By staying abreast of these developments, you can proactively adapt your strategies and protect your financial assets. Remember, knowledge is power, and informed decision-making is the cornerstone of long-term financial success.

Another vital aspect of this ongoing journey is the art of consistent review and refinement. Regularly reviewing your financial plan is critical to ensure it's still aligned with your goals and circumstances.

Life throws unexpected curveballs – job changes, unexpected expenses, family additions – which may necessitate adjustments to your budget, investment strategy, or retirement plan. This ongoing review process helps you stay on track, identify areas needing improvement, and make timely corrections to maintain your financial stability.

For instance, a change in career might require reassessing your savings goals, adjusting your investment portfolio, or modifying your retirement plan. Unexpected medical expenses could

necessitate revisiting your emergency fund and exploring insurance options. Similarly, the arrival of children might necessitate

adjustments in your spending habits, childcare arrangements, and future education planning. Regularly analyzing your financial situation and adapting your plan accordingly demonstrates financial prudence and ensures you stay on the path toward long-term

success.

Furthermore, maintaining a healthy relationship with money is crucial for sustained financial wellbeing. This involves fostering a mindset of mindful spending, conscious investing, and responsible debt management. Avoiding impulsive purchases, sticking to your budget, and strategically managing debt are vital for long-term financial stability. Avoid getting caught up in the consumerist culture that constantly promotes instant gratification. Instead, cultivate the discipline to save and invest regularly, prioritizing long-term goals over immediate desires. This involves mindful spending habits, which entail making informed decisions rather than impulsive purchases. Analyze your spending patterns to understand where your money goes. Look for ways to reduce unnecessary expenses and allocate funds towards savings and investments.

Beyond personal finances, consider the broader societal and environmental impact of your financial decisions. Sustainable investing is gaining popularity, and more and more investors are aligning their portfolios with their values. This includes investing in businesses committed to environmental responsibility, social justice, and ethical practices. These investments may not always provide the highest returns, but they contribute to a better world and align your financial choices with your personal beliefs. This also extends to supporting local businesses, reducing your carbon footprint, and making conscious consumer choices that promote sustainability.

Another significant aspect of the ongoing financial journey is the importance of giving back. As you achieve greater financial stability, consider contributing to causes that resonate with you. Philanthropy isn't just about large donations; it's about giving back in ways that align with your values. This could involve volunteering time, donating to a charity, or supporting a local cause. The act of giving back is not only fulfilling but can also provide a sense of purpose and deeper satisfaction beyond personal financial gains.

It's also important to actively engage in continuous learning and personal development to maintain momentum in your financial journey. The world of finance is dynamic, and new information and trends continually emerge. Staying informed and adapting your strategies accordingly is crucial. Seek out educational resources, attend workshops, or connect with financial professionals to enhance your knowledge and skills. This proactive approach ensures you remain ahead of the curve and make informed financial decisions.

Building strong financial habits is vital. Creating a budget, monitoring expenses, saving consistently, and investing wisely are key aspects of building a secure financial future. These habits help you maintain financial discipline, making it easier to manage

expenses and reach your financial goals. Financial literacy plays a critical role in your financial journey. Understanding concepts such as budgeting, saving, investing, and debt management can empower you to make informed choices, avoid pitfalls, and achieve financial success.

Throughout your journey, remember the importance of goal-setting. Clearly defined financial goals provide direction and motivation, helping you stay focused and make progress. Regularly reviewing and adjusting your goals as your circumstances change is essential.

This ensures your financial plan remains aligned with your

aspirations and life stages. Remember that your goals may evolve over time. Perhaps you'll want to buy a house, pay off student loans, start a family, or pursue further education. Adapting your plan based on these evolving needs is vital to maintain progress.

Finally, remember that the journey to financial success is not a race; it is a marathon that requires patience, discipline, and a long-term perspective. Embrace the learning process, celebrate milestones along the way, and maintain a positive attitude. The rewards of achieving financial freedom are immense, not only in terms of financial security but also in terms of peace of mind and the ability to live life on your own terms. Embrace the ongoing journey and relish the ongoing rewards it offers. The true measure of success is not just the accumulation of wealth, but the journey of growth, learning, and positive impact that it creates. And in this ongoing journey, remember that financial success is not a destination, but a continuous process of adaptation, growth, and learning. It's about building resilience, embracing change, and staying committed to your long-term financial wellbeing.

Glossary

This glossary provides definitions for key financial terms used throughout the book. For more in-depth explanations, refer to the relevant chapters.

Asset: Something you own that has value.

Liability: Something you owe money on.

Net Worth: The difference between your assets and liabilities.

Budget: A plan for how you will spend your money.

Emergency Fund: Savings set aside for unexpected expenses.

Investing: Putting money into assets with the expectation of earning a return.

Diversification: Spreading your investments across different asset classes to reduce risk.

Compounding: Earning interest on your interest.

Debt: Money you owe to others.

Interest: The cost of borrowing money.

Financial Literacy: Understanding of financial concepts and how to manage money effectively.

Sustainable Investing: Investing in companies that prioritize environmental, social, and governance (ESG) factors.

Author Biography

Killian Drake is a millennial personal finance expert and coach with a proven track record of helping young adults achieve financial success. Having personally navigated the challenges of early-career finances and debt, Khalid Dawood brings a unique blend of

practical experience and empathetic understanding to their work. They leverage their background in non-fiction writing and a deep understanding of financial principles to empower others to take control of their financial futures. He is passionate about

demystifying personal finance and making it accessible to everyone, regardless of their background or starting point. Beyond their coaching work, Khalid Dawood regularly contributes to various financial publications and speaks at workshops and conferences. Their mission is to inspire and guide individuals on their journeys toward financial freedom, offering tools, strategies, and ongoing support to help them build a secure and fulfilling financial future.

Don't miss out!

Visit the website below and you can sign up to receive emails whenever Killian Drake publishes a new book. There's no charge and no obligation.

https://books2read.com/r/B-A-JAYLD-CCQBG

BOOKS 2 READ

Connecting independent readers to independent writers.

www.ingramcontent.com/pod-product-compliance
Lightning Source LLC
LaVergne TN
LVHW052257200926
848481LV00002B/395